OSCOLA

The Oxford University Standard for Citation of Legal Authorities

Fifth Edition

Faculty of Law, University of Oxford
www.law.ox.ac.uk/oscola

Contents

Introduction 1

1 General notes 3

   1.1 Citations and footnotes 3
       1.1.1 Citing cases 3
       1.1.2 Citing legislation 4
       1.1.3 Citing secondary sources 5
       1.1.4 Order of sources in footnotes 5
       1.1.5 Indicators 5

   1.2 Subsequent citations, cross-references and Latin 'gadgets' 6
       1.2.1 Subsequent citations 6
       1.2.2 Cross-references 7
       1.2.3 Latin 'gadgets' 8

   1.3 Punctuation, ranges of numbers and years, and words
       in other languages 8
       1.3.1 Punctuation 8
       1.3.2 Ranges of numbers and years 8
       1.3.3 Words in other languages 8

   1.4 Foreign sources 9
   1.5 Quotations 9
   1.6 Lists of abbreviations and tables 11
       1.6.1 Lists of abbreviations 11
       1.6.2 Tables of cases 11
       1.6.3 Tables of legislation and other tables 12

   1.7 Bibliographies 12

2 Primary Sources 14

   2.1 Cases from England and Wales (including the Supreme
       Court and Privy Council) 14
       2.1.1 General principles 14
       2.1.2 Case names 15
       2.1.3 Medium neutral citations 18
       2.1.4 Law reports 18
       2.1.5 Courts 19
       2.1.6 Pinpoints 20
       2.1.7 Judges' names 20

		2.1.8	Subsequent history of a case	22

- 2.1.8 Subsequent history of a case 22
- 2.1.9 Cases decided before 1865 22

2.2 Cases from Scotland 23
- 2.2.1 Medium neutral citations and law reports 23
- 2.2.2 Judges' names 24

2.3 Cases from Northern Ireland 25
- 2.3.1 Medium neutral citations and law reports 25
- 2.3.2 Judges' names 25

2.4 UK primary legislation 25
- 2.4.1 Names of statutes 25
- 2.4.2 Parts of statutes 26
- 2.4.3 Older statutes 26
- 2.4.4 Explanatory notes to statutes 27
- 2.4.5 Bills 27
- 2.4.6 Wales 27
- 2.4.7 Scotland 28
- 2.4.8 Northern Ireland 28
- 2.4.9 Assimilated European Union law 29

2.5 UK secondary legislation 29
- 2.5.1 Statutory instruments 29
- 2.5.2 Parts of statutory instruments 30
- 2.5.3 Rules of court 30
- 2.5.4 Wales 31
- 2.5.5 Scotland 31
- 2.5.6 Northern Ireland 31

2.6 Cases and legislation from other jurisdictions 31
- 2.6.1 Cases 31
- 2.6.2 Legislation 32

3 Secondary sources 33

3.1 General principles 33
- 3.1.1 Authors' names 33
- 3.1.2 Titles 33
- 3.1.3 Pinpoints 33
- 3.1.4 Electronic sources 33
- 3.1.5 Subsequent citations 34

3.2 Books 34
- 3.2.1 Authored books 34
- 3.2.2 Ebooks 35
- 3.2.3 Edited and translated books 35
- 3.2.4 Contributions to edited books 35
- 3.2.5 Older works 36

		3.2.6	Books of authority and institutional works 36
		3.2.7	Encyclopedias 36
		3.2.8	Dictionaries 37
	3.3	Articles 37
	3.4	Case notes 38
	3.5	Book reviews 38
	3.6	Working papers 39
	3.7	Other secondary sources 39
		3.7.1	Websites 39
		3.7.2	Podcasts 40
		3.7.3	Lectures and speeches 40
		3.7.4	Interviews 41
		3.7.5	Conference papers 41
		3.7.6	Theses 41
		3.7.7	Newspaper articles 41
		3.7.8	*Hansard* and parliamentary reports 42
		3.7.9	Command papers 42
		3.7.10	Other government publications 43
		3.7.11	Law Commission reports and papers 43
		3.7.12	Personal communications 44
		3.7.13	Generative artificial intelligence 44
4	International sources 45
	4.1	Treaties 45
		4.1.1	General principles 45
		4.1.2	Treaty reservations and declarations 47
		4.1.3	WTO/GATT agreements and related official documents 47
	4.2	United Nations documents 48
		4.2.1	UN Charter 48
		4.2.2	General principles 48
		4.2.3	United Nations Yearbooks and Official Records 49
		4.2.4	International Law Commission materials 49
		4.2.5	United Nations agencies 50
		4.2.6	United Nations treaty bodies 50
	4.3	International cases and decisions 51
		4.3.1	International Court of Justice and Permanent Court of Justice 51
		4.3.2	International Tribunal for the Law of the Sea 53
		4.3.3	International Criminal Court and ad hoc criminal tribunals 53

		4.3.4	WTO/GATT decisions..54

      4.3.5 International arbitral and other tribunal decisions.................54
      4.3.6 Other materials of international courts and tribunals...........55

  4.4 Regional materials 56

      4.4.1 European Union legislation..56
      4.4.2 Court of Justice of the European Union and General Court decisions 58
      4.4.3 European Commission materials 58
      4.4.4 European Court of Human Rights decisions 59
      4.4.5 European Commission of Human Rights decisions 60
      4.4.6 Inter-American Court of Human Rights decisions.................60
      4.4.7 Other regional courts and tribunals...60
      4.4.8 Other materials of regional bodies..60

  4.5 Other international sources...61

      4.5.1 General principles..61
      4.5.2 International Yearbooks..61
      4.5.3 International Law Association and Institut de Droit International documents 61
      4.5.4 Collected Courses of the Hague Academy of International Law...62
      4.5.5 International law digests 62
      4.5.6 Max Planck Encyclopedias of International Law 62

5 Appendix...63

  5.1 Guide to medium neutral citations 63

      5.1.1 United Kingdom 63
      5.1.2 England and Wales 63
      5.1.3 Scotland..63
      5.1.4 Northern Ireland 64
      5.1.5 Tribunals 64

  5.2 Abbreviations 65

      5.2.1 Abbreviations of the names of law reports, journals and treaty series 65
      5.2.2 Abbreviations used in legal historical works.........................68
      5.2.3 Abbreviations of the titles of books of authority 68
      5.2.4 Abbreviations in case names 68
      5.2.5 Abbreviations of common words and phrases in footnotes...69
      5.2.6 Abbreviations of international institutions and bodies 70

  5.3 Guides for other jurisdictions 71

  5.4 Other useful sources..72

Index..73

Introduction

The *Oxford University Standard for Citation of Legal Authorities* ('OSCOLA') was devised by Peter Birks in 2000, in consultation with students and academics at the Oxford Law Faculty. Subsequent editions of OSCOLA were produced in 2002 (by Peter Birks), in 2004 (by Timothy Endicott and Sandra Meredith) and in 2012 (by Donal Nolan and Sandra Meredith). This new edition of OSCOLA provides more detailed coverage of domestic legal sources and reinstates a heavily revised version of the treatment of international law sources which was included in the early editions of OSCOLA. There are two golden rules for the citation of legal authorities. One is consistency. The other is consideration for the reader. Legal writing is more persuasive when the author refers to legal materials in a consistent and familiar way. OSCOLA is designed to help the author to achieve consistency and to make life easier for the reader. We hope that OSCOLA continues to show the consideration for authors and readers that motivated Professor Birks to devise a uniform standard for citation of legal authorities.

In preparing this edition, the following methodological principles were adopted. First, we generally resisted the temptation to make changes to the prescriptions of the fourth edition. Adjusting the rules comes at a cost, namely, that users of OSCOLA need to learn and implement the new guidance. Expecting users to incur this cost is unjustified unless changing course would yield significant benefits to either users of OSCOLA or readers of their works. Second, we have not laid down rules that deal with every single issue that arises in connection with legal citation. Had we done so, the length of OSCOLA would have ballooned and its accessibility would have been compromised. This means that some citation issues, typically those which arise infrequently or only in specialised contexts, have simply been left to the common sense of OSCOLA's users to resolve. Third, given the extent to which OSCOLA has been adopted, we embarked on a substantial consultation exercise and the responses thereto informed our work. We are grateful to the following participants in this exercise: Alexandros Antoniou, Charlie Brampton, Katie Cox, Catherine Dale, Kate Faulkner, Emily Finch, Laura Griffiths, Julius Grower, Jackie Hanes, Rachel Hogg, Hilary Johnson, Charles Knight, Wendy Lynwood, Paul Magrath, Claire Mazer, Richard Pears, Alex Pooley, OSCOLA Ireland, Lee Snook, William Swadling, Hester Swift, Matt Thomson, Joy Tilley, Stephen Ward, Suzanne White and Richard Wong.

Numerous other debts of gratitude are owed in connection with the present edition. We are particularly grateful to Lucy Cameron, Sophie Ryan and Yuxin Wang, who provided excellent research assistance. Elizabeth Wells was an invaluable source of advice. We particularly wish to thank in connection with international law sources Anna-Mira Brandau, the members of the editorial board of the *Cambridge International Law Journal*, Natasha Holcroft-Emmess, Angus Johnston, Eleni Methymaki, Lung Wan Pun, Peter Tzeng, Priya Urs, Philippa Webb and Anna Ventouratou. We had useful correspondence with LexisNexis regarding retained/assimilated European Union legislation and have been influenced by the guidance that LexisNexis developed. Andrew Dickinson and Johannes Ungerer also provided constructive comments in this connection. We are grateful to Michael Lobban for helping in relation to historical sources. Václav Janeček provided excellent input regarding generative artificial intelligence. Joseph Crampin provided invaluable guidance as to best practice with respect to the problem of 'link rot'. Wilson Liu gave assistance as regards Hong Kong materials. Finally, we would like to thank Hart Publishing for agreeing to publish OSCOLA while allowing us to continue to make the online version available free of charge from the OSCOLA website.

James Goudkamp (Editor)

Donal Nolan (Consultant Editor)

17 December 2025

Feedback regarding OSCOLA would be gratefully received and should be sent to oscola@law.ox.ac.uk.

The OSCOLA website (https://www.law.ox.ac.uk/oscola) provides further information regarding OSCOLA, such as answers to frequently asked questions and links to previous editions.

1 General notes

1.1 Citations and footnotes

When citing a source, place the reference in a footnote. Indicate footnotes with a superscript number. The footnote marker should be positioned at the end of the sentence unless, for the sake of clarity, it is necessary to put it directly after the word or phrase to which it relates. The marker should always be placed after any punctuation save that where the marker relates to parenthetical text it should be placed within the brackets. Close footnotes with a full stop (or question or exclamation mark). Where more than one citation is given in a single sentence in a footnote, separate them with semi-colons. Footnotes should be consecutively numbered save in the case of longer works such as books and theses where the footnote numbering should restart for each chapter of the work.

> In *Patel v Mirza*,[59] the Supreme Court overhauled the law regarding the defence of illegality. That case, which was preceded by two Supreme Court decisions, *Hounga v Allen*[60] and *Les Laboratoires Servier v Apotex Inc*,[61] in which inconsistent approaches to the defence were taken, has been heralded as a landmark in the law of unjust enrichment.[62] (Subsequent case law makes it clear that *Patel* applies across private law more generally.[63])
>
> [59] [2016] UKSC 42, [2017] AC 467.
> [60] [2014] UKSC 47, [2014] 1 WLR 2889.
> [61] [2014] UKSC 55, [2015] AC 430.
> [62] See Andrew Burrows, 'A New Dawn for the Law of Illegality' in Sarah Green and Alan Bogg (eds), *Illegality after Patel v Mirza* (Hart Publishing 2018).
> [63] *Grondona v Stoffel & Co* [2020] UKSC 42, [2021] AC 540; *Henderson v Dorset Healthcare University NHS Foundation Trust* [2020] UKSC 43, [2021] AC 563.

1.1.1 Citing cases

When citing cases, give the name of the case (unless it is given in the text) followed by the medium neutral citation (if any). If the case is reported, the reference to the best report should be supplied after the medium neutral citation (section 2.1.4). Where no medium neutral citation is available, a court identifier should be given (section 2.1.5). Retrospectively created medium neutral citations should not be used. This means that medium neutral citations that predate 2001 should be disregarded.

> In *Robinson v Chief Constable of West Yorkshire Police*,[31] the Supreme Court clarified the law regarding the duty of care element of the tort of negligence. In particular, it explained that the tripartite test associated with the decision in *Caparo Industries plc v Dickman*[32] should no longer be used.
>
> [31] [2018] UKSC 4, [2018] AC 736.
> [32] [1990] 2 AC 605 (HL).

'Pinpoints' give the page or paragraph number of the judgment (or report of the judgment) to which the reader is being referred. The inclusion of pinpoints is essential (particularly when quoting) except when reference is being made to a case as a whole as in relation to both of the cases cited in the previous example. In the next example, footnote 19 contains a pinpoint reference to a page whereas footnote 20 contains a pinpoint reference to a paragraph. Where paragraph numbers are available, they should be used in preference to page numbers. Paragraph numbers, unlike page numbers, should be placed within square brackets.

> In *Roe v Minister of Health*, Denning LJ observed that 'you will find that the three questions, duty, causation, and remoteness, run continually into one another'.[19] However, in *Darnley v Croydon Health Services NHS Trust*, Lord Lloyd-Jones warned against eliding the breach element of a claim for the tort of negligence with the duty element.[20]
>
> [19] [1954] 2 QB 66 (CA) 86.
> [20] [2018] UKSC 50, [2019] AC 831 [21].

It is generally unnecessary to identify the judge to whose judgment reference is made except when quoting from the judgment and the identity of the judge is not clear from the text. When it is necessary to identify the judge, place the judge's name in brackets at the end of the citation.

> [1] *Sevilleja v Marex Financial Ltd* [2020] UKSC 31, [2021] AC 39 [3] (Lord Reed).

1.1.2 Citing legislation

When referring to legislation, it is unnecessary to give a citation in a footnote if all the information that the reader needs about the source is provided in the text, as in the following sentence.

> This case highlights the far-reaching judicial role ushered in by the Human Rights Act 1998.

Conversely, where the text does not include the name of the source or the relevant provision, this information should be provided in a footnote. When citing legislation in a footnote, it is unnecessary to preface the reference with the definite article 'the'.

British courts must only consider Strasbourg jurisprudence: they are not bound by it.¹

¹ Human Rights Act 1998, s 2.

1.1.3 Citing secondary sources

If relying on or referring to a secondary source, such as a book or an article, provide a citation for the work in a footnote.

> Hart wrote that the doctrine of precedent is compatible with 'two types of creative or legislative activity': *distinguishing* the earlier case by 'narrowing the rule extracted from the precedent' and *widening the rule* by discarding 'a restriction found in the rule as formulated from the earlier case'.³⁴
>
> ³⁴ HLA Hart, *The Concept of Law* (2nd edn, Clarendon Press 1994) 135.

1.1.4 Order of sources in footnotes

When citing more than one source of the same kind for a single proposition, put the sources in chronological order. Separate the citations with semi-colons, and do not precede the final citation with 'and'. However, if one or more of the sources are more directly relevant than the others, cite it (or these) first, and then cite the less relevant ones in a new sentence, beginning with the indicator 'See also'. If citing legislation and case law for a single proposition, refer to the legislation before the cases, and if citing primary and secondary sources for a single proposition, cite the primary sources before the secondary ones.

> ¹ FH Newark, 'The Boundaries of Nuisance' (1949) 65 LQR 480; Richard Kidner, 'Nuisance and Rights of Property' [1998] Conv 267; Ken Oliphant, 'Unblurring the Boundaries of Nuisance' (1998) 6 Tort L Rev 21; Paula Giliker, 'Whither the Tort of Nuisance? The Implications of Restrictions on the Right to Sue in *Hunter v Canary Wharf*' (1999) 7 Torts LJ 155.
>
> ² *Brent v Haddon* (1619) Cro Jac 555, 79 ER 476; *Broder v Saillard* (1876) 2 Ch D 692 (Ch); *Pemberton v Bright* [1960] 1 All ER 792 (CA). See also *Torette House Pty Ltd v Berkman* (1939) 62 CLR 637 (HCA).
>
> ³ Social Action, Responsibility and Heroism Act 2015, s 4; Allen M Linden, 'Rescuers and Good Samaritans' (1971) 34 MLR 9.
>
> ⁴ Defamation Act 2013, s 1(1); *Lachaux v Independent Print Ltd* [2019] UKSC 27, [2020] AC 612 [12]–[17], [20]–[26].

1.1.5 Indicators

Indicators are words or abbreviations that precede a citation and which assist the reader to understand why you are giving it. Common indicators include 'See also', 'cf', 'eg' and 'ie'. 'See also' means that the source in issue is an additional one which readers should consult for more detail. 'cf' is an abbreviation for the Latin word *confer*, which means compare. 'eg' is an abbreviation for 'for example'. 'ie' is an abbreviation for 'that is'. Never italicise indicators or capitalise the first letter thereof, even when they appear at the start of a sentence. An exception to this rule concerns the indicator 'See also', which should be presented as shown in footnote 1 in the example below. Indicators should not be followed by any punctuation.

> ¹ Tarunabh Khaitan and Sandy Steel, 'Theorizing Areas of Law: A Taxonomy of Special Jurisprudence' (2022) 28 LEG 325. See also Stephen A Smith, *Contract Theory* (OUP 2004) ch 1.
> ² Adrienne Stone, 'Unconstitutional Constitutional Amendments: Between Contradiction and Necessity' (2018) 12 Vienna J Intl Const L 357; cf Yaniv Roznai, *Unconstitutional Constitutional Amendments* (OUP 2017) 105–22.
> ³ eg Constitutional Reform and Governance Act 2010, s 2.
> ⁴ ie the Constitutional Reform Act 2005.
> ⁵ cf Donal Nolan, 'Deconstructing the Duty of Care' (2013) 129 LQR 559.

1.2 Subsequent citations, cross-references and Latin 'gadgets'

1.2.1 Subsequent citations

In a subsequent citation of a source, briefly identify the source and provide a cross-citation in brackets to the footnote in which the full citation can be found. 'ibid' should not be used. In the case of longer works, citations should begin afresh for each chapter.

EXAMPLE of subsequent citation of a case

In this example, a citation for *Austin v Commissioner of Police for the Metropolis* is provided in footnote 1. As the name of the case is given in the text, it is not given in the footnote (section 1.1.1). The second citation at footnote 2 gives a short form of the case name and the cross-citation to the full citation. It also pinpoints several paragraphs in the case.

> ¹ [2009] UKHL 5, [2009] AC 564.
> ² *Austin* (n 1) [34], [39], [43]–[47].

EXAMPLE of subsequent citation of legislation

This example shows legislation for which a short form could be used in a subsequent citation. The short form is indicated at the end of the full citation and can be used without a cross-citation to the full citation.

> ³² Social Action, Responsibility and Heroism Act 2015 ('SARAH') s 1.
>
> …
>
> ⁴⁰ SARAH, s 2.
> ⁴¹ SARAH, s 3.

EXAMPLE of subsequent citation of a book

This example shows a citation of a book which is first cited (in full) in footnote 1 and then cited again in footnotes 26 and 27 by way of a cross-citation to footnote 1.

> [1] Robert Stevens, *Torts and Rights* (OUP 2007).
>
> ...
>
> [26] Stevens (n 1) 110.
>
> [27] Stevens (n 1) 219.

EXAMPLE of subsequent citation of two works by the same author

This example shows how to cite two works by the same author subsequent to their initial citation.

> [1] Rebecca Williams, 'Accountable Algorithms: Adopting the Public Law Toolbox Outside the Realm of Public Law' (2022) 75 CLP 237.
>
> ...
>
> [5] Rebecca Williams, 'Rethinking Administrative Law for Algorithmic Decision Making' (2021) 42 OJLS 468.
>
> ...
>
> [26] Williams (n 1) 240.
>
> [27] Williams (n 5) 472.

EXAMPLE of subsequent citation of two works by the same author which appear in a single footnote

In this example, two different works by the same author are cited in a single footnote. The subsequent citations give the author's surname and the title of the work or a short form thereof.

> [27] Andrew Ashworth, 'Testing Fidelity to Legal Values: Official Involvement and Criminal Justice' (2000) 63 MLR 633, 635; Andrew Ashworth, *Positive Obligations in Criminal Law* (Hart Publishing 2013) 68.
>
> ...
>
> [35] Ashworth, 'Testing Fidelity to Legal Values' (n 27) 635–37.
>
> ...
>
> [46] Ashworth, *Positive Obligations in Criminal Law* (n 27) 73.

1.2.2 Cross-references

Cross-references direct the reader to discussion elsewhere in your work. Avoid sending the reader off to another part of the text when a short point could easily be restated. Never use a cross-reference that will make it difficult for the reader to locate the text to which you are referring, such as simply 'See above'. A good cross-reference takes the reader straight to the very place to which they are being directed, for example, 'See n 109' (which invites the reader to read footnote 109) or

'See text to n 20' (which asks the reader to refer to the text that accompanies the marker to footnote 20).

> As argued above,[20] the objective standard of care in the tort of negligence is pregnant with the risk of causing unfairness to the defendant. The courts, however, sanction the use of the objective standard on practical grounds.[21]
>
> [20] See text to n 10.
> [21] See n 12.

1.2.3 Latin 'gadgets'

Avoid the use of Latin 'gadgets' such as *ibid*, *supra*, *infra*, *ante*, *id*, *op cit*, *loc cit* and *contra*, some of which are not widely understood and several of which cause certain difficulties arising from, for example, autocorrect functions in word processors. It is, however, permissible to use the Latin abbreviations 'eg', 'ie' and 'cf' (section 1.1.5).

1.3 Punctuation, ranges of numbers and years, and words in other languages

1.3.1 Punctuation

OSCOLA uses minimal punctuation. For example, abbreviations and initials in authors' names do not take full stops, *Weekly Law Reports* is cited as 'WLR' and the 'Director of Public Prosecutions' is abbreviated to 'DPP'.

> [1] *Malcolm v DPP* [2007] EWHC 363 (Admin), [2007] 1 WLR 1230.
> [2] JG Fleming, 'Remoteness and Duty: The Control Devices in Liability for Negligence' (1953) 31 Can Bar Rev 471.

1.3.2 Ranges of numbers and years

When referring to ranges of numbers, use both figures for numbers between ten and twenty, and thereafter use as few figures as possible (for example, write 1–6, 11–17, 121–221 and 1782–812). This is subject to three qualifications. First, always use at least two digits for the final number (thus, write 1782–83 rather than 1782–3). Second, where the final number would otherwise start with a '0', give an additional digit (thus, write 201–203 rather than 201–03). Third, ranges of paragraph numbers should never be truncated. For example, write [120]–[123] rather than [120]–[23]. If the range of numbers indicates years, and the years span centuries, give the final year in full (for example, write 1871–1914, 1925–27, 1965–75 and 1989–2001).

1.3.3 Words in other languages

In the text, italicise words and phrases in languages other than the one in which you are writing, unless they form part of a quotation. Provide a translation immediately afterwards in brackets, or in a footnote, if doing so is likely to assist the reader. However, if writing in English, do not italicise foreign words and phrases that are in common usage in legal English, such as 'cy-près', 'ultra vires', 'stare decisis', 'obiter dicta', 'ratio decidendi', 'a priori' and 'a fortiori'. Commonly used Latin abbreviations, such as 'cf', 'ie' and 'eg', are not italicised (section 1.1.5).

1.4 Foreign sources

When referring to foreign materials, cite primary sources as in their home jurisdiction, with the exception that full stops in abbreviations should be dropped. Guides for other jurisdictions can be found in section 5.3 of the appendix. Cite secondary sources in accordance with the OSCOLA rules governing the citation of secondary sources.

1.5 Quotations

Use single inverted commas to denote quotations, except quotations within quotations, which take double inverted commas. Quotations must be faithful to the original, except where it is necessary to change quotation marks from single to double, or vice versa. Any errors in the original should be marked by writing '[sic]' immediately after the error. Incorporate quotations of up to three lines into the text. If a quotation is incorporated into the text, then no more than a comma (at most) is required to introduce it. Punctuation follows the closing quotation mark, unless it is an essential part of the quotation, as a question or exclamation mark might be. The footnote marker comes last, after both the closing quotation mark and the punctuation.

> The Chief Justice explained that this power 'is not limited to defence against aggression from a foreign nation'.[41]
>
> …
>
> Brian Bix raises the question, 'What is the point of a dissent, after all, at least on the highest court of the jurisdiction, if the law simply is whatever the majority on that court says it is?'[62]

Present quotations that are longer than three lines in an indented paragraph, with no further indentation of the first line. Leave a line space above and below the indented quotation. In the case of indented quotations, do not use quotation marks, except for single quotation marks to denote any quotations within the quotation. When intervening text is omitted from the quotation, or if it ends mid-sentence in the original text, use an ellipsis ('…') to indicate that some of the original text is missing. Never use an ellipsis at the start of a quotation. Leave a space between an ellipsis and any text or punctuation.

> As Andrew Ashworth observed:
>> [T]he House of Lords … concluded that the civil standard of proof … should be applied in such a way as to be sensitive to the 'seriousness of the matters to be proved and the implications of

> proving them', which in effect means proof beyond reasonable doubt (ie the criminal standard).²⁷
>
> ²⁷ Andrew Ashworth, 'Social Control and "Anti-Social Behaviour"': The Subversion of Human Rights' (2004) 120 LQR 263, 276, citing *Clingham and McCann* [2002] UKHL 39, [2003] 1 AC 787 [83] (Lord Hope).

When it is necessary to attribute a quotation or citation within a quotation to its original source, omit the footnote marker from the original text in your quotation, and give the original author's citation in your footnote.

> Mark Elliott, Jack Williams and Alison Young observe that 'the Supreme Court expressly praised the blogosphere in its judgment: "The very full debate in the courts has been supplemented by a vigorous and illuminating academic debate conducted on the web (particularly through the UK Constitutional Law Blog site)".⁹⁹
>
> ⁹⁹ Mark Elliott, Jack Williams and Alison L Young, 'The Miller Tale: An Introduction' in Mark Elliott, Jack Williams and Alison L Young (eds), *The UK Constitution After Miller: Brexit and Beyond* (Hart Publishing 2018) 24, citing *R (Miller) v Secretary of State for Exiting the European Union* [2017] UKSC 5, [2018] AC 61 [274] (Lord Carnwath).

If it is not necessary to attribute such a quotation or citation because it is either implicit or irrelevant, omit the footnote markers or citations and add '(footnotes omitted)' or '(citations omitted)' as applicable after the citation in your own footnote.

> The authors conclude 'the notion that the notification issued by the UK to the European Council on 29 March 2017 is invalid ... seems hard to sustain'.¹⁰¹
>
> ¹⁰¹ Elliot, Williams and Young (n 99) 27 (footnote omitted).

If you add emphasis to a quotation, write '(emphasis added)' after the citation. Conversely, if the emphasis was in the original quotation put '(emphasis in original)' after the citation.

> In *Transfield Shipping Inc v Mercator Shipping Inc (The Achilleas)*, Lord Hoffmann reasoned as follows:
>
>> It seems to me logical to found liability for damages upon the intention of the parties (objectively ascertained) because all contractual liability is voluntarily undertaken. It must be in principle wrong to hold someone liable for risks for which people entering into such a contract *in their particular market*, would not reasonably be considered to have undertaken.¹²
>
> ¹² [2008] UKHL 48, [2009] 1 AC 61 [12] (emphasis added).

1.6 Lists of abbreviations and tables

A longer work, such as a book or a thesis, generally has in the preliminary pages a list of abbreviations and tables of all the cases, legislation and other primary legal sources cited in the work. Shorter works, such as articles and essays, only require footnotes. The list of abbreviations should come before the tables. As concerns the order of the tables, the table of cases should generally come first, followed by the table of legislation, followed by other tables.

1.6.1 Lists of abbreviations

In an article or essay, it will sometimes be in the interests of both precision and avoiding repetition to define certain terms. This can be done either in a footnote or in the text.

> This point is illustrated in the Law Commission's report on the illegality defence in 2010 ('the 2010 Report').[21]
>
> [21] Law Commission, *The Illegality Defence* (Law Com No 320, 2010) para 3.12.

However, in a book or thesis, it might be more convenient to define unfamiliar abbreviations in a list of abbreviations in the preliminary pages. Do not define abbreviations that are part of everyday legal usage, such as 'DPP'. For lists of common abbreviations that need not be defined, see section 5.2 of the appendix.

1.6.2 Tables of cases

In a table of cases, case names are not italicised. Unless there are very few cases, divide the table into separate sections for different jurisdictions. Cases should be listed in alphabetical order of first significant word in the name of the case. For instance, *Re Farquar's Estate* should be tabled as 'Farquar's Estate, Re'. Cases identifying parties by initial only should be listed under the initial. For example, *Re F (mental patient: sterilisation)* becomes 'F (mental patient: sterilisation), Re'. When listing cases with names such as *R v Smith* in works on criminal law, dispense with the 'R' and list the case as 'Smith', but if citing such cases in a work primarily concerned with another area of law, list them by their full names, under 'R', and also do this when citing judicial review cases in which the Crown is the first-named party.

List trademark cases and shipping cases under the full case name, but insert an additional entry in the table under the trademark or the name of the ship (again using the first significant word, so that *The Starsin* becomes 'Starsin, The'), with a cross-reference to the full name (the indicator for which should be italicised).

> Starsin, The. *See* Homburg Houtimport BV v Agrosin Private Ltd

List European Union ('EU') court decisions alphabetically by case name and state the case number in round brackets before providing the European Case Law Identifier.

> Schempp v Finanzamt (Case C-403/03) EU:C:2005:446

Tables of cases must be indexed in order that the reader can locate the pages of the work where the cases are mentioned.

> A v Bottrill [2002] UKPC 44, [2003] 1 AC 449 163
> AB v South West Water Services Ltd [1993] 2 WLR 507 (CA)...... 57, 301
> Abacrombie & Co, Re [2008] EWHC 2520 (Ch)..................................... 84
> Abbar v Saudi Economic & Development Co (SEDCO) Real Estate Ltd
> [2013] EWHC 1414 (Ch).. 91
> Addis v Gramophone Co Ltd [1909] AC 488 (HL)................................ 99

1.6.3 Tables of legislation and other tables

Tables of legislation and other tables, such as tables of international treaties, should follow the table of cases. A table of legislation should list every statute cited in the work, with the entry for each statute being sub-divided to show where which parts of the statute (sections, subsections and so on) are cited. Statutory instruments should be listed separately, at the end of the list of statutes. If there are a large number of citations of statutory instruments, it may be helpful to have wholly separate tables of statutes and statutory instruments. In tables of legislation, legislation should be listed in alphabetical order of first significant word of the title. If legislation from more than one jurisdiction is cited, it may be helpful to have separate lists for each jurisdiction. Tables of legislation and other tables must be indexed.

> Carriage by Air Act 1961 93
>   s 1.. 93
>   sch 1B, art 29.. 93
> Competition Act 1988 110
>   s 36.. 110
> Consumer Protection Act 1987... 24
> Consumer Rights Act 2015... 29
>   s 47C(1) 29

1.7 Bibliographies

In longer works, such as theses and books, a bibliography listing secondary sources should be provided after the main body of text and any appendices (primary sources do not need to be included since they will be captured by the tables at the start of the work). It need not be indexed. Items in bibliographies take the same form as other citations in OSCOLA, with three exceptions. First, the author's surname should precede his or her initial(s), with no comma separating the surname from the initial(s), but a comma after the final initial. Second, initials should be used instead of forenames. Third, the titles of unattributed works should be preceded by a double em-dash. Works should be arranged in alphabetical order of author surname, with unattributed works being listed at the beginning of the bibliography in alphabetical order of first major word of the title. It is unnecessary to separate the various types of secondary sources from each other. In other words, a bibliography does not require separate sections for (for instance) books and articles. Entries in bibliographies should not end with a full stop.

CITATION in a footnote

> ¹ Elizabeth Fisher, *Risk Regulation and Administrative Constitutionalism* (Hart Publishing 2007).

CITATION in a bibliography

> Fisher E, *Risk Regulation and Administrative Constitutionalism* (Hart Publishing 2007)

If citing several works by the same author in a bibliography, list the author's works in chronological order (starting with the oldest), and in alphabetical order of first major word of the title within a single year. After the citation of the first work, replace the author's name with a double em-dash. Place works by more than one author under the first-named author's name, but after that author's sole-authored works. If a first-named author has more than one co-author, arrange the co-authored works in alphabetical order of co-author surname, and if you are citing more than one work by the same first-named author and co-author, arrange the works in chronological order, repeating the co-author's name each time.

> Hart HLA, *Law, Liberty and Morality* (OUP 1963)
> —— 'Varieties of Responsibility' (1967) 83 LQR 346
> —— *Punishment and Responsibility* (OUP 1968)
> —— and Honoré AM, *Causation in the Law* (OUP 1959)
> —— and Honoré AM, *Causation in the Law* (2nd edn, OUP 1985)

2 Primary Sources

2.1 Cases from England and Wales (including the Supreme Court and Privy Council)

2.1.1 General principles

The components of a typical case citation are the case name, the medium neutral citation and the reference to the best report of the case.

> *case name* | [year] | court | number, | [year] | volume | report abbreviation | first page
>
> OR
>
> *case name* | [year] | court | number, | (year) | volume | report abbreviation | first page

The case name should be italicised. The rest of the citation should not be italicised. A comma separates the medium neutral citation and the law report citation. There are no full stops in the abbreviations. For example, write 'UKHL' rather than 'U.K.H.L.' and 'AC' rather than 'A.C.'

The example below indicates that the case between Corr and IBC Vehicles Ltd was the thirteenth judgment handed down by the House of Lords in 2008, and that a report of the judgment can be found in volume one for 2008 of the series of the *Law Reports* called the *Appeal Cases*, beginning at page 884.

> [1] *Corr v IBC Vehicles Ltd* [2008] UKHL 13, [2008] 1 AC 884.

Medium neutral citations are a modern development, so many case citations consist only of the case name and the reference to the report. The components of a typical case citation without a medium neutral citation are as follows:

> *case name* | [year] | volume | report abbreviation | first page | (court identifier)
>
> OR
>
> *case name* | (year) | volume | report abbreviation | first page | (court identifier)

As the following example shows, when the year is used to identify the law report volume it is given in square brackets. Where the year is necessary to identify the volume and there is more than one volume in a year, give the year in square brackets and the volume number before the report abbreviation. If there is only a single volume for the year in issue, there is no need to include the volume number.

> 1 *Page v Smith* [1996] AC 155 (HL).
> 2 *Barrett v Enfield LBC* [2001] 2 AC 550 (HL).

Give the year of the law report volume in round brackets when the volumes of the series in issue are independently numbered. In other words, the year should be placed within round brackets when it is possible to identify the volume of the report in issue by reference to the volume number alone.

> 1 *R v East Sussex CC, ex p Ward* (2000) 3 CCL Rep 132 (QBD).
> 2 *S (a child) v Birmingham HA* (2001) 58 BMLR 66 (QBD).

2.1.2 Case names

Where there are multiple claimants or defendants, name only the first claimant and first defendant. Where the parties are individuals, omit their forenames and initials. Abbreviate common words and phrases. Thus, use '*BC*' for '*Borough Council*', '*Co*' for '*Company*', '*DPP*' for '*Director of Public Prosecutions*' and so on (see section 5.2.4 of the appendix for more abbreviations). Use '*Re*' in preference to '*In the matter of*', '*In re*' and so on. For instance, write '*Re the Companies Act 1985*' rather than '*In the matter of the Companies Act 1985*' and '*Re Farquar's Estate*' instead of '*In re the Estate of Farquar*'. Abbreviate '*ex parte*' to '*ex p*'. The '*p*' has no full stop. Do not include expressions such as '*and another*' or '*and ors*'. Omit descriptions such as '*a firm*' if the party in question is named, but if only the initial of the party is provided, then the description (such as '*a minor*') should be given. Also omit (in old Scottish cases) the maiden names of married women (for example, write '*Bourhill v Young*', not '*Hay v Young*' or '*Bourhill (Hay) v Young*'. If only the initial or initials of the party are provided, then they should be used. Terms indicating corporate status (such as '*Ltd*', '*plc*' and '*LLC*') should be included in the citation if part of the heading of the report.

> 1 *R v Environmental Agency, ex p Turnbull* [2000] Env LR 715 (QBD).
> 2 *Re A (Children) (Conjoined Twins: Surgical Separation)* [2001] Fam 147 (CA).
> 3 *Re Bernard L Madoff Investment Securities LLC* [2009] EWHC 442 (Ch), [2010] BCC 328.
> 4 *Emerald Supplies Ltd v British Airways plc* [2009] EWHC 741 (Ch), [2010] Ch 48.
> 5 *Cardiff and Vale University Health Board v T (a minor)* [2019] EWHC 1671 (Fam).
> 6 *IIXA v Surrey CC* [2023] UKSC 52, [2024] 1 WLR 335.

Short forms of case names
Give the name of the case in full when it is first mentioned in the text or footnotes; it may be shortened thereafter. Thus, '*Phelps v Hillingdon LBC*' can be shortened to

'*Phelps*' (example 1). If a case name is shortened in this way, the name chosen must be that which stands first in the full name of the case. In shipping cases, the name of the ship can be used instead of the full case name (example 2). It is common in works on criminal law to see 'in *R v Caldwell*' shortened to 'in *Caldwell*', even in the first citation, but less so where a small number of criminal cases are cited in a work primarily concerned with another area of law. Either form is acceptable (example 3). A like approach also applies in the tax context, where it is only the name of the taxpayer that differentiates cases from each other (example 4). Popular names for cases may also be used. Give the popular name in brackets and inverted commas after the initial full citation, and then use the popular name in subsequent citations (example 5).

EXAMPLE 1

[14] *Phelps v Hillingdon LBC* [2001] 2 AC 619 (HL).

...

[19] *Phelps* (n 14).

EXAMPLE 2

[25] *Leigh & Sillivan Ltd v Aliakmon Shipping Co Ltd (The Aliakmon)* [1986] AC 785 (HL).

...

[45] *The Aliakmon* (n 25).

EXAMPLE 3

[11] *R v Evans* [2009] EWCA Crim 650, [2009] 1 WLR 13 OR *Evans* [2009] EWCA Crim 650, [2009] 1 WLR 13.

...

[23] *R v Evans* (n 11) OR *Evans* (n 11).

EXAMPLE 4

[89] *HMRC v Tooth* [2021] UKSC 17, [2021] 3 All ER 711 OR *Tooth* [2021] UKSC 17, [2021] 3 All ER 711.

...

[101] *HMRC v Tooth* (n 89) OR *Tooth* (n 89).

EXAMPLE 5

[12] *Mirage Studios v Counter-feat Clothing Co Ltd* [1991] FSR 145 (Ch D) ('*Ninja Turtles case*').

...

[15] *Ninja Turtles case* (n 12).

Judicial review applications
Judicial review applications decided before 2001 are cited as follows:

> ¹ *R v Lord Chancellor, ex p Witham* [1998] QB 575 (QBD).
> ...
> ⁵ *Witham* (n 1) 576.

For cases decided from 2001 onwards, the following form is used:

> ¹ *R (Roberts) v Parole Board* [2004] EWCA Civ 1031, [2005] QB 410.
> ...
> ¹⁰ *Roberts* (n 1) 410.

Attorney General's references
For the case name in Attorney General's references, give the number or numbers of the reference and the year in brackets. If there is a name associated with the reference, it should follow at the end of the case name, also in brackets. '*Attorney General*' can be abbreviated to '*A-G*' in subsequent references.

> ¹ *Attorney General's Reference (No 3 of 2004) (R v H)* [2005] EWCA Crim 1882.
> ² *Attorney General's Reference (Nos 56, 57 and 58 of 2008)* [2009] EWCA Crim 235, [2009] 2 Cr App R (S) 52.

Variations in the name of a case
Where the same case is reported under significantly different names in different law reports, use the name given in the heading of the report being cited. Where two or more reports using different names are cited, the report or reports using the alternative name of the case should be introduced by the phrase 'sub nom' (an abbreviation of '*sub nominee*', meaning 'under the name').

> ¹ *Gibbons v South West Water Services Ltd* [1993] QB 507, sub nom *AB v South West Water Services Ltd* [1993] 2 WLR 507 (CA).

Similarly, where a case appears under a different name at different stages in its history (that difference in the name being more than a mere reversal of the names of the parties), and both stages are being cited, the name of the case at the second stage cited should be introduced by 'sub nom'.

> ¹ *R v Monopolies and Mergers Commission, ex p South Yorkshire Transport Ltd* [1992] 1 WLR 291 (CA), affd sub nom *South Yorkshire Transport Ltd v Monopolies and Mergers Commission* [1993] 1 WLR 23 (HL).

2.1.3 Medium neutral citations

In 2001, the House of Lords, Privy Council, Court of Appeal and Administrative Court began issuing judgments with a medium neutral citation which identified the judgment independently of any report. This practice was extended to all divisions of the High Court in 2002, and later to tribunals and commissions. Transcripts of judgments with medium neutral citations are often available on the British and Irish Legal Information Institute website (www.bailii.org) and the National Archives 'Find Case Law' database (https://caselaw.nationalarchives.gov.uk). The cases are numbered consecutively throughout the year and all cases with medium neutral citations have numbered paragraphs. A list of medium neutral citations is provided in sections 5.1.1 and 5.1.2 of the appendix.

Medium neutral citations give the year of judgment, the court and the judgment number. The court is not included in brackets at the end of a medium neutral citation because the medium neutral citation itself identifies it. However, medium neutral citations from the High Court include a court identifier in brackets after the judgment number. Where a judgment with a medium neutral citation has not been reported, give only the medium neutral citation. Where such a judgment has been reported, give the medium neutral citation followed by a citation of the best report (section 2.1.4), separated by a comma. Medium neutral citations that have been devised for cases decided prior to the introduction of medium neutral citations should never be used.

> [1] *Corr v IBC Vehicles Ltd* [2008] UKHL 13, [2008] 1 AC 884.
> [2] *Farraj v Kings NHS Healthcare Trust* [2009] EWCA Civ 1203, [2010] 1 WLR 2139.
> [3] *Court v Despalliers* [2009] EWHC 3340 (Ch), [2010] 2 All ER 451.
> [4] *R (Mahfoud) v Secretary of State for the Home Department* [2010] EWHC 2057 (Admin).

If a single report includes more than one judgment and therefore more than one medium neutral citation, list the medium neutral citations in chronological order, starting with the oldest, and separate them with a comma.

> [1] *Masterman-Lister v Brutton & Co (Nos 1 and 2)* [2002] EWCA Civ 1889, [2003] EWCA Civ 70, [2003] 1 WLR 1511.

2.1.4 Law reports

A law report is a published report of a judgment, with additional features such as a headnote summarising the facts of the case and the judgment, catchwords used for indexing and lists of cases considered.

The 'best report'

The *Law Reports* series published by the Incorporated Council of Law Reporting (www.iclr.co.uk) are the most authoritative. Different series of the *Law Reports* cover judgments of the House of Lords/Supreme Court and Privy Council (known as *Appeal Cases*), the Chancery Division, the Family Division, the King's/Queen's Bench Division and so on. These reports include a summary of the arguments of counsel.

If a case is reported in the *Law Reports*, this report should be cited in preference to any other report. If a judgment is not reported in the *Law Reports*, cite the *Weekly Law Reports* or the *All England Law Reports*. Only if a judgment is not reported in one of these general series should you refer to a specialist series, such as the *Lloyd's Law Reports* or the *Family Law Reports*.

Heavily edited reports

Where a report of a case gives only a summary or a heavily edited version of the judgment (which is the norm for reports in newspapers and some practitioner journals), cite the report only if there is no medium neutral citation and no other, fuller, report.

> [1] *Taylor v Glass* [1979] CLY 672 (CA).
> [2] *Quainoo v Brent and Harrow AHA* (1982) 132 NLJ 1100 (QBD).
> [3] *Powick v Malvern Wells Water Co* The Times, 28 September 1993 (QBD).

Unreported cases

If a case is unreported but has a medium neutral citation, give that citation. If an unreported case does not have a medium neutral citation (which will always be the case before 2001), give the court and the date of the judgment in brackets after the name of the case. There is no need to add the word 'unreported'.

> [1] *Stubbs v Sayer* (CA, 8 November 1990).
> [2] *Calvert v Gardiner* [2002] EWHC 1394 (QB).

Reports using case numbers in the citation

Volume 4 of the *Weekly Law Reports*, which is published only online, uses case numbers rather than page numbers. Similarly, in some specialist law reports, cases are given case numbers which run consecutively through the volumes, rather than page numbers. Examples include the *Reports of Patent, Design and Trademark Cases*, the *Criminal Appeal Reports* and the *Personal Injuries and Quantum Reports*. In such cases, follow the citation method used by the series in question.

> [1] *Rozario v Post Office* [1997] PIQR P15 (CA).
> [2] *Thompson Holidays Ltd v Norwegian Cruise Lines Ltd* [2002] EWCA Civ 1828, [2003] RPC 32.
> [3] *R v Kelly* [2008] EWCA Crim 137, [2008] 2 Cr App R 11.
> [4] *Re G* [2022] EWFC 55, [2023] 4 WLR 27.

2.1.5 Courts

Cases which lack a medium neutral citation require a court identifier unless they were decided before 1865. Use 'HL' for the House of Lords, 'PC' for the Privy Council,

'CA' for the Court of Appeal, and 'KBD', 'QBD', 'Ch D' and 'Fam' for the divisions of the High Court. Court identifiers should come at the end of the citation save that they should appear before any pinpoint.

> [1] *Donoghue v Stevenson* [1932] AC 562 (HL).
> [2] *Goldman v Hargrave* [1967] 1 AC 645 (PC).
> [3] *Froom v Butcher* [1976] QB 286 (CA).
> [4] *JEB Fasteners Ltd v Marks, Bloom & Co* [1981] 3 All ER 289 (QBD).
> [5] *Corporacion Nacional del Cobre de Chile v Sogemin Metals Ltd* [1997] 1 WLR 1396 (Ch D).
> [6] *Re KR (a child) (Abduction: Forcible Removal by Parents)* [1999] 4 All ER 954 (Fam).

2.1.6 Pinpoints

A pinpoint is a reference to a particular paragraph of a judgment or page of a report. If the judgment has numbered paragraphs, pinpoint to a particular paragraph by putting the relevant paragraph number in square brackets. The pinpoint should come at the end of the citation, including after any report. If pinpointing to more than one paragraph, separate the paragraph numbers with a comma. If citing spans of paragraphs, insert an en-dash between the first and last paragraph being cited.

> [1] *Callery v Gray* [2001] EWCA Civ 1117, [2001] 1 WLR 2112 [42], [45].
> [2] *Bunt v Tilley* [2006] EWHC 407 (QB), [2006] 3 All ER 336 [1]–[37].

If a case citation ends with a court identifier in brackets, the pinpoint follows the identifier, without any comma preceding it. Where the pinpoint reference is to the first page of the report, repeat the page number. Multiple pinpoints to pages should be separated by commas.

> [1] *Beattie v E & F Beattie Ltd* [1938] Ch 708 (CA) 720, 723.
> [2] *R v Leeds County Court, ex p Morris* [1990] 1 QB 523 (QBD) 530–31.

If an unreported judgment does not have paragraph numbers, pinpoint to the relevant page of the judgment.

> [1] *Ryde Holdings Ltd v Rainbow Corp Ltd* (PC, 15 November 1993) 3.

2.1.7 Judges' names
When referring to a judge, do so according to the table below.

Judicial Office	Abbreviation
Baron	Smith B
Chancellor of the High Court	Sir John Smith C/Dame Jane Smith C
Chief Baron	Smith CB

Judicial Office	Abbreviation
Circuit Court Judge	HHJ Smith (although if the judge is a King's Counsel, write HHJ Smith KC)
County Court Judge	HHJ Smith (although if the judge is a King's Counsel, write HHJ Smith KC)
Deputy Judge of the High Court	Mr John Smith/Mrs Jane Smith (although if the Deputy Judge is a King's Counsel, write Mr John Smith KC/Mrs Jane Smith KC)
District Judge	Smith DJ
Judge of the High Court	Smith J
Judge of the Insolvency and Companies Court	ICC Judge Smith
Justice of the Supreme Court (including the President and Deputy President)	Lord/Lady Smith
Lord Chancellor	Lord Smith LC
Lord/Lady Chief Justice	Lord/Lady Smith CJ
Lord/Lady Justice of Appeal (including Presidents of Divisions)	Smith LJ
Lord of Appeal in Ordinary	Lord/Lady Smith
Master of the High Court	Master Smith
Master of the Rolls	Smith MR (unless a peer, in which case write Lord/Lady Smith MR)
Vice-Chancellor	Smith V-C

Forenames are not used unless there are two judges with the same surname, in which case both the forename and surname of the junior judge of the two is given (for example, 'Geoffrey Lane LJ'). If a judge is a peer and has a rank higher than that of Baron or Baroness, the higher rank is used (for example, 'Viscount Dilhorne'). Omit a Law Lord's territorial qualification (accordingly, write 'Lord Scott' rather than 'Lord Scott of Foscote'). Retired judges who still hear cases are referred to by their name and title, for example, 'Sir John Smith'. If a judge was elevated to a new appointment after the decision in the case you are citing, use the title of the judge at that time (there is no need to add the words 'as he/she then was'). If referring to more than one judge of the High Court or the Court of Appeal, use the abbreviations 'JJ' or 'LJJ' respectively. However, do not write 'Lords Smith and Jones' when referring to two Law Lords. Instead, you should write 'Lord Smith and Lord Jones'. When pinpointing to a particular passage in a judgment, add the judge's name in brackets after the pinpoint.

EXAMPLES in the text

> Lord Woolf CJ rejected this argument because ...
>
> This is evident from the decision in *Horncastle*, in which Lord Phillips said ...
>
> Rimer and Pill LJJ were of the opinion that ...
>
> As Tugendhat J pointed out in *Ajinomoto Sweeteners* ...

EXAMPLES in footnotes

> [1] *Crown River Cruises Ltd v Kimbolton Fireworks Ltd* [1996] 2 Lloyd's Rep 533 (QB) 547 (Potter J); *Graham and Graham v ReChem International Ltd* [1996] Env LR 158 (QB) 162 (Forbes J); *Arscott v The Coal Authority* [2004] EWCA Civ 892, [2005] Env LR 6 [27] (Laws LJ).

2.1.8 Subsequent history of a case

The subsequent history of a case may be indicated after the primary citation by abbreviating 'affirmed' to 'affd' and 'reversed' to 'revd'.

> [1] *Roberts v Gable* [2006] EWHC 1025 (QB), [2006] EMLR 23, affd [2007] EWCA Civ 721, [2008] QB 502.

2.1.9 Cases decided before 1865

The English Reports

More than 100,000 'nominate reports' of judgments handed down before 1865 are reprinted in a series called the *English Reports*. If a judgment is reprinted in the *English Reports*, you should give the citations in both the nominate report and the *English Reports*, divided by a comma (unless there is a pinpoint, in which case by a semi-colon).

> [1] *Boulton v Jones* (1857) 2 H&N 564, 157 ER 232.
> [2] *Henly v Mayor of Lyme* (1828) 5 Bing 91, 107; 130 ER 995, 1001.

Other older cases

Party names in cases in the ecclesiastical courts should be separated by '*c*' rather than '*v*'.

> [1] *James c Harmon* (1514) 101 SS 24.

Where reported legal argument in a single case in a single court extends over several years, the date format (1621–23) may be used. Where the year of a case is uncertain, but must fall between two known years, use the format (1621×1623).

Yearbook references should be formatted as follows:

> (calendar year) | YB | term | regnal year, | folio, | plea number

> ¹ (1400) YB Mich 2 Hen IV, fo 3v, pl 9.

The Rolls Series, Selden Society, Ames Foundation and legal history sourcebooks should be checked for better reports and translations. For example, the case cited above as an example of yearbook citation could also be cited as follows:

> ¹ *Wootton v Brgeslay* (1400) JH Baker, *Baker & Milsom Sources of English Legal History: Private Law to 1750* (2nd edn, OUP 2019) 422.

Cases dating from the yearbook period, and not reported in the Maynard edition of the yearbooks, can be found in the Rolls Series yearbooks ('RS') (Edward I and part of Edward III), in the Selden Society yearbooks series ('SS') (Edward II and some outliers), in the Ames Foundation yearbooks series ('AF') (Richard II), in separately published books or in manuscript. Where a case is reported in one of the three alternative yearbook series, give the party names, the year in brackets and the source. Anonymous cases should be cited in the same way, but without the parties' names.

> ¹ *Helton v Kene* (1344) YB 18 & 19 Edw III, RS p 194.
> ² *Petstede v Marreys* (1310) YB 3 & 4 Edw II, 22 SS vol 29.
> ³ *Skyrne v Butolf* (1388) YB Pas 11 Ric II, AF p 223, pl 12.

Cases reported in separately published books should be cited by the parties' names (if available), followed by the year in brackets and then the book reference and page number, as in the example from *Baker & Milsom Sources of English Legal History* given above. Cases in manuscript should be cited by party names (if available), followed by the year in brackets and then the standard reference for the manuscript source.

> ¹ *Blake v Lynch* (1743) Lincoln's Inn Nill MS 79, p 134.

Standard abbreviations used in legal historical works are provided in section 5.2.2 of the appendix.

2.2 Cases from Scotland

2.2.1 Medium neutral citations and law reports

In 2005, the superior Scottish courts began providing medium neutral citations. Medium neutral citations follow the model used in England and Wales. The forms of medium neutral citation for the different Scottish courts are listed in section 5.1.3 of the appendix.

The most authoritative series of law reports in Scotland is *Session Cases*. The single periodical *Session Cases* contains separately paginated sequences of reports from the Court of Session ('SC'), the High Court of Justiciary ('JC') and the House of Lords/Supreme Court ('SC (HL)' or 'SC (UKSC)'). Before 1906, volumes of *Session Cases* were cited by editor and volume number: the editors were Shaw (S), Dunlop (D), Macpherson (M), Rettie (R) and Fraser (F).

Refer to *Session Cases* if possible. The next most authoritative series of law reports is the *Scots Law Times* (SLT), which is also arranged in separately paginated sequences of reports from different courts. With the exception of reports from the superior courts, the section is indicated in brackets following the abbreviation SLT. Other law reports series in Scotland include the *Scottish Civil Law Reports* (SCLR) and the *Scottish Criminal Case Reports* (SCCR).

Citations to judgments of the Court of Session should indicate whether the case was heard in the Inner House or Outer House by adding (IH) or (OH) after the citation. In citations of Scottish law reports, the year is not put in brackets if it is required to locate the case in the series of reports, but it is put in round brackets if the volumes of the report series are independently numbered. Pinpoint in the same way as for cases from England and Wales.

1 *Hislop v Durham* (1842) 4 D 1168.
2 *Adams v Advocate General* 2003 SC 171 (OH) 175.
3 *Dodds v HM Advocate* 2003 JC 8 (JC).
4 *Davidson v Scottish Ministers* [2005] UKHL 74, 2006 SC (HL) 41 [10].
5 *Smart v HM Advocate* [2006] HCJAC 12, 2006 JC 119 [23]–[24].
6 *Ponticelli Ltd v Gallagher* [2023] CSIH 32, 2023 SLT 823.

2.2.2 Judges' names
When referring to a judge, do so according to the table below.

Judicial Office	Abbreviation
Head of Sheriffdom	Sheriff Principal Smith
Judge of the Sheriff Appeal Court	Appeal Sheriff Smith
Judge of the Sheriff Court	Sheriff Smith (although if presiding over a summary matter, use Summary Sheriff Smith)
Lord Justice Clerk and President of the Second Division of the Court of Session	Lord Justice Clerk
Lord President of the Court of Session and Lord Justice General of Scotland	For civil matters, Lord President; for criminal matters, Lord Justice General
Senator of the College of Justice sitting in the Supreme Courts (the Court of Session or the High Court of Justiciary)	Lord/Lady Smith
Temporary judge of the Supreme Courts	Judge Smith

2.3 Cases from Northern Ireland

2.3.1 Medium neutral citations and law reports
The Northern Ireland jurisdiction dates from 1921, and the *Northern Ireland Law Reports* from 1925. For cases decided before 1925, cite the *Irish Reports* or the *Irish Times Reports*. Medium neutral citations follow the model used in England and Wales. The forms of medium neutral citation for the different Northern Irish courts are listed in section 5.1.4 of the appendix. Court identifiers should be supplied where there is no medium neutral citation.

> [1] *Hylands v McClintock* [1999] NI 28 (Ch D).
> [2] *Wilson v Commissioner of Valuation* [2009] NICA 30, [2010] NI 48.

2.3.2 Judges' names
When referring to a judge, do so according to the table below.

Judicial Office	Abbreviation
County Court Judge	HHJ Smith (although if the judge is a King's Counsel, write HHJ Smith KC)
District Judge	Smith DJ
Judge of the High Court	Smith J
Lord/Lady Chief Justice	Lord/Lady Smith CJ
Lord/Lady Justice of Appeal	Smith LJ
Master of the High Court	Master Smith

2.4 UK primary legislation

2.4.1 Names of statutes
Cite an Act by its short title and year using capitals for the first letter of major words and without a comma before the year. The title of the statute should not be italicised. The definite article 'the' should not feature in references to statutes unless the statute is being discussed within a sentence, in which case it will generally be necessary to include the definite article in order to form a coherent sentence.

> [1] Act of Supremacy 1558.
> [2] Shipping and Trading Interests (Protection) Act 1995.

If several jurisdictions are discussed in a work, it may be necessary to add the jurisdiction of the legislation in brackets at the end of the citation.

> [1] Water Resources Act 1991 (UK).
> [2] Civil Liability Act 2002 (NSW).

2.4.2 Parts of statutes

Statutes are divided into parts, sections, subsections, paragraphs and subparagraphs. In addition, the main text of the statute may be supplemented by schedules, which are divided into paragraphs and subparagraphs. The relevant abbreviations are as follows:

part/parts	pt/pts
section/sections	s/ss
subsection/subsections	sub-s/sub-ss
paragraph/paragraphs	para/paras
subparagraph/subparagraphs	subpara/subparas
schedule/schedules	sch/schs

In the text, cite legislation as follows:

EXAMPLES in the text

> Section 5(1)(a) of the Race Relations Act 1976 provides …
>
> As discussed above, s 11(1A) of the Limitation Act 1980 …
>
> … as provided by ss 1(2) and 7(2) …
>
> Subsection (1) does not apply to …
>
> … as sub-s (3) shows …

In footnotes, insert a comma after the year, and a space between the relevant abbreviation and the part of the Act being cited.

EXAMPLES in footnotes

> [16] Criminal Attempts Act 1981, ss 1(1) and 4(3).
> [17] Sexual Offences Act 2003, s 1(1)(c).

2.4.3 Older statutes

For older statutes, it may be helpful to give the regnal year and chapter number. In the example below, the information in brackets indicates that the Act was given royal assent in the forty-first year of the reign of George III. The abbreviation 'c' stands for chapter. The Crown Debts Act 1801 was the ninetieth Act to receive royal assent in that session of Parliament, and so is chapter 90.

> [1] Crown Debts Act 1801 (41 Geo 3 c 90).

2.4.4 Explanatory notes to statutes

When citing explanatory notes to statutes, precede the name of the statute with the words 'Explanatory Notes to the ...'. When pinpointing, cite the paragraph number(s), preceded by 'para(s)'.

> [1] Explanatory Notes to the Charities Act 2006, para 15.

2.4.5 Bills

Cite a bill by its title, the House in which it originated, the Parliamentary session in round brackets and the running number assigned to it. Running numbers for House of Commons Bills are put in square brackets; those for House of Lords Bills are not. When a Bill is reprinted at any stage it is given a new running number.

> title | HC Bill | (session) | [number]
>
> OR
>
> title | HL Bill | (session) | number

Refer to parts of Bills applying the rules that govern the citation of parts of statutes (section 2.4.2). The abbreviations for 'clause' and 'clauses' are 'cl' and 'cls'.

> [1] Consolidated Fund HC Bill (2008–2009) [5].
> [2] Academies HL Bill (2010–11) 1, cl 8(2).

2.4.6 Wales

Acts (post-2011)

Acts of the Welsh Parliament (Senedd Cymru) are cited by short title and year. When citing in English, insert an 'asc' number in brackets, consisting of a lowercase abbreviation of the words 'Act of Senedd Cymru' and a running number in the year (eg, 'asc 2'). When citing in Welsh, use the lowercase abbreviation 'dsc' with the running number in the year (eg, 'dsc 2'). Acts of the National Assembly for Wales are cited in the same way save that the abbreviation should be 'anaw' ('dccc' in Welsh). Cite parts of Welsh Acts in the same format as for parts of UK Parliament statutes (section 2.4.2).

> [1] Deddf Trawsblannu Dynol (Cymru) 2013 (dccc 5).
> [2] Child (Abolition of Defence of Reasonable Punishment) (Wales) Act 2020 (anaw 3).
> [3] Welsh Tax Acts etc (Power to Modify) Act 2022 (asc 2).

Measures (pre-2011)

Measures of the National Assembly for Wales made prior to 2011 are cited by short title and year. When citing in English, insert a 'nawm' number in brackets, consisting of a lowercase abbreviation of the words 'National Assembly of Wales Measure' and a running number in the year (eg, 'nawm 2'). When citing in Welsh, use the lowercase abbreviation 'mccc' with the running number in the year (eg, 'mccc 2').

> [1] Learner Travel (Wales) Measure 2008 (nawm 2).
> [2] Mesur Teithio gan Ddysgwyr (Cymru) 2008 (mccc 2).

Bills

Bills of the Welsh Parliament are cited by short title, the stage of progress in square brackets and the year.

> [1] Agriculture (Wales) Bill [as amended at Stage 2] 2020.
> [2] Bil Diogelu'r Amgylchedd (Cynhyrchion Plastig Untro) (Cymru) [fel y'i cyflwynwyd] 2022.

2.4.7 Scotland

Acts

Acts of the Scottish Parliament are cited by short title and year. Each Act is also given an 'asp' number, consisting of a lowercase abbreviation of the words 'Act of the Scottish Parliament' and a running number in the year (eg, 'asp 13'). The asp number should be given after the year, in brackets. Cite parts of Acts of the Scottish Parliament in the same format as for parts of UK Parliament statutes (section 2.4.2).

> [1] Crofting Reform etc Act 2007 (asp 7).

Bills

Bills before the Scottish Parliament are cited by Scottish Parliament Bill number and title, followed by the stage of progress in square brackets, the session and the year in round brackets. Unlike UK Parliament Bills, Scottish Parliament Bills retain their original numbering throughout, with amended versions of the Bill being identified by an alphabetical suffix.

> [1] SP Bill 4 Abolition of Feudal Tenure etc (Scotland) Bill [as introduced] Session 1 (1999).
> [2] SP Bill 4A Abolition of Feudal Tenure etc (Scotland) Bill [as amended at Stage 2] Session 1 (2000).

2.4.8 Northern Ireland

Acts

When citing Acts of the former Parliament of Northern Ireland, put 'NI' in brackets between the short title and the year. When citing Acts of the current Northern Ireland Assembly, which was established in 1998, put 'Northern Ireland' in brackets between the short title and the year.

> ¹ Poultry Improvement Act (NI) 1968.
> ² Presumption of Death Act (Northern Ireland) 2009.

Bills

Bills before the Northern Ireland Assembly are cited by short title, the stage of progress in square brackets and the year, with 'Northern Ireland' between the short title and the stage of progress.

> ¹ Budget Bill (Northern Ireland) [as introduced] 2020.
> ² Welfare Supplementary Payments (Amendment) Bill (Northern Ireland) [as amended at further consideration stage] 2022.

2.4.9 Assimilated European Union law

The citation of EU materials is addressed in section 4.4.1. When citing direct EU legislation that has been assimilated into UK law pursuant to the European Union (Withdrawal) Act 2018 and the Retained EU Law (Revocation and Reform) Act 2023, differentiate the assimilated UK version by adding the word 'Assimilated' before the title of the legislation and replace the OJ reference with a reference to any amending UK statutory instruments. The title of the assimilated UK version of EU legislation should be provided as it appears in the assimilated UK version.

An example of a citation of direct EU legislation, with a short form provided at the end, is as follows:

> ¹ Regulation (EC) No 593/2008 of the European Parliament and of the Council of 17 June 2008 on the law applicable to contractual obligations [2008] OJ L177/6 ('Rome I Regulation (EU)').

An example of a citation of the assimilated UK version of the same direct EU legislation, with a short form provided at the end, is as follows:

> ¹ Assimilated Regulation (EC) No 593/2008 of the European Parliament and of the Council of 17 June 2008 on the law applicable to contractual obligations, as amended by SI 2019/834, reg 10 ('Rome I Regulation (Assimilated)').

2.5 UK secondary legislation

2.5.1 Statutory instruments

Statutory instruments (orders, regulations and rules) are numbered consecutively throughout the year. The year combines with the serial number to provide an SI number that follows the abbreviation 'SI' and which is used to identify the legislation. When citing a statutory instrument, give the name, year and (after a comma) the SI number.

> [1] Penalties for Disorderly Behaviour (Amendment of Minimum Age) Order 2004, SI 2004/3166.
>
> [2] Russia (Sanctions) (EU Exit) Regulations 2019, SI 2019/855.

Statutory instruments used to be called statutory rules and orders, and these are cited by their title and SR & O number.

> [1] Hollow-ware and Galvanising Welfare Order 1921, SR & O 1921/2032.

2.5.2 Parts of statutory instruments

The rules for referring to parts of statutory instruments mirror those for referring to parts of statutes (section 2.4.2). In addition to those given above for parts of statutes, use the following abbreviations:

article/articles	art/arts
regulation/regulations	reg/regs
rule/rules	r/rr

> [1] Eggs and Chicks (England) Regulations 2009, SI 2009/2163, reg 7(2).

2.5.3 Rules of court

The Civil Procedure Rules ('CPR') (and their predecessors, the Rules of the Supreme Court ('RSC') and the County Court Rules ('CCR')), the Criminal Procedure Rules ('CrPR') and Family Procedure Rules ('FPR') should be cited without reference to their SI number or year.

> [1] CPR 5.2(1)(b).
> [2] CPR 7.1.
> [3] RSC Ord 24 r 14A.
> [4] CCR Ord 17 r 11.
> [5] CrPR 8.4.
> [6] FPR 15.2.

Practice Directions ('PD') accompanying the CPR, the CrPR and FPR are referred to by number, according to the part they supplement.

> [1] CPR PD 7.
> [2] CPR PD 52C.
> [3] CrPR PD 1.
> [4] FPR PD 2A

2.5.4 Wales
Statutory instruments of the Welsh Parliament are cited in the same way as other statutory instruments, but the SI number is followed by a Welsh SI number, in brackets. Statutory instruments made at Westminster that apply to Wales are cited in the same way as UK statutory instruments (sections 2.5.1 and 2.5.2).

> [1] Learner Travel (Wales) Measure 2008 (Commencement No 2) Order, SI 2009/2819 (W 245).
> [2] Gorchymyn Mesur Teithio gan Ddysgwyr (Cymru) 2008 (Cychwyn Rhif 2) SI 2009/2819 (Cy 245).

2.5.5 Scotland
Statutory instruments of the Scottish Parliament are cited in the same way as other statutory instruments, but the number takes the abbreviation 'SSI'. Acts of Sederunt and Acts of Adjournal should be cited in the same way as other statutory instruments, with SI or SSI being used as appropriate. Statutory instruments made at Westminster that apply to Scotland are cited in the same way as UK statutory instruments (sections 2.5.1 and 2.5.2).

> [1] Act of Adjournal (Criminal Appeals) 2003, SSI 2003/387.
> [2] Plant Health (EU Exit) Scotland (Amendment) (No 2) Regulations 2021, SSI 2021/489.
> [3] Act of Sederunt (Lands Valuation Appeal Court) 2023, SSI 2023/75.

2.5.6 Northern Ireland
Northern Ireland statutory rules, which are the equivalent of statutory instruments, are made by the Northern Ireland Executive or the Northern Ireland Office. Cite the short title and year, followed by the SR number. Statutory instruments made at Westminster that apply to Northern Ireland are cited in the same way as UK statutory instruments (sections 2.5.1 and 2.5.2).

> [1] Rates (Regional Rates) Order (Northern Ireland) 2022, SR 2022/50.

2.6 Cases and legislation from other jurisdictions

2.6.1 Cases
Cite cases from other jurisdictions as they are cited in their own jurisdiction, but with minimal punctuation. If the name of the law report series cited does not itself indicate the court, you should also give this in either full or short form in brackets at the end of the citation. When citing a decision of the highest court of a US state, the abbreviation of the name of the state suffices.

> [1] *Henningsen v Bloomfield Motors Inc* 161 A 2d 69 (NJ 1960).
> [2] *Roe v Wade* 410 US 113 (1973).
> [3] *Waltons Stores (Interstate) Ltd v Maher* (1988) 164 CLR 387 (HCA).
> [4] *Harriton v Stephens* [2006] HCA 15, (2006) 226 CLR 52.
> [5] BGH NJW 1992, 1659.
> [6] Cass civ (1) 21 January 2003, D 2003, 693.
> [7] CA Colmar 25 January 1963, Gaz Pal 1963.I.277.
> [8] *Brown v New Zealand Basing Ltd* [2018] 1 NZLR 245 (SC).
> [9] *Government of the City of Buenos Aires v HN Singapore Pte Ltd* [2023] SGHC 139.
> [10] *Kerr v Baranow* 2011 SCC 10, [2011] 1 SCR 269.
> [11] *Re Lam Kwok Hung Guy, ex p Tor Asia Credit Master Fund LP* [2023] HKCFA 9, (2023) 26 HKCFAR 119.

2.6.2 Legislation

Cite legislation from other jurisdictions as it is cited in its own jurisdiction, but without any full stops in abbreviations. Give the jurisdiction if necessary in brackets.

> [1] Accident Compensation Act 1972 (NZ).
> [2] *loi n° 75-1349 du 31 décembre 1975 relative à l'emploi de la langue française*.
> [3] 1976 Standard Terms Act (*Gesetz über Allgemeine Geschäftsbedingungen*) (FRG).
> [4] COVID-19 Emergency Response Act (SC 2020 c 5).
> [5] Climate Change Act 2022 (Cth).

Guides for citations from other jurisdictions can be found in section 5.3 of the appendix.

3 Secondary sources

3.1 General principles

3.1.1 Authors' names
Give the author's name exactly as it appears in the publication but omit titles and postnominals (such as 'KC'). For website and social media content, the author's name is their username. If there are more than three authors, give the first author's name followed by 'and others'. If no individual author is identified, but an organisation or institution claims editorial responsibility for the work, then cite it as the author. If no person, organisation or institution claims responsibility for the work, begin the citation with the title. Treat editors' names in the same way as authors' names.

3.1.2 Titles
Italicise the titles of books and similar publications, including all publications with ISBNs. The titles of all other works should be placed within single inverted commas and not italicised. Capitalise the first letter in all major words in a title. Minor words, such as 'for', 'and', 'or' and 'the', do not take a capital letter unless they begin the title or subtitle.

3.1.3 Pinpoints
Pinpoints to parts, chapters, pages and paragraphs come at the end of the citation. Use 'pt(s)' for 'part(s)', 'ch(s)' for 'chapter(s)', and 'para(s)' for 'paragraph(s)'. Page numbers stand alone, without 'p' or 'pp'. When referring to pages, give a specific page or range of pages. Pinpoints to electronic video or audio content, such as YouTube videos or podcasts, should include references to the timestamp of the relevant content where available (see sections 3.7.1–3.7.2). Separate minutes and seconds with a colon. When referring to a timespan, give a range (eg, 14:14–18:30). When referring to a footnote, give the page or paragraph pinpoint where the footnote marker is located, followed by the footnote number, which should be preceded by 'fn'.

> [1] Mark Leeming, *Common Law, Equity and Statute: A Complex Entangled System* (Federation Press 2023) 9 fn 6.

3.1.4 Electronic sources
If you source a publication online which is also available in hard copy (which is the case for most books and journals), cite only the hard copy version. Electronic sources should be cited in accordance with section 3.7.1.

3.1.5 Subsequent citations

Subsequent citations and short form names should follow the guidance given in section 1.2.1.

3.2 Books

Cite all publications with an ISBN as if they were books, whether they are read online or in hard copy. Older books do not have ISBNs but should be cited as books even if read online.

3.2.1 Authored books

Cite the author's name first, followed by a comma, and then the title of the book in italics (sections 3.1.1 and 3.1.2). Where a book has a title and subtitle not separated with punctuation, insert a colon. Publication information follows the title within brackets. Publication elements should always include the publisher and the year of publication, with a space but no punctuation between them. The place of publication need not be given. If you are citing an edition other than the first edition, indicate that within the brackets using the form '2nd edn' (or 'rev edn' for a revised edition). Additional information should be of a clarifying nature: it may include, for example, the supplement number.

> author, | *title* | (additional information, | edition, | publisher | year)

> [1] JG Fleming, *The Law of Torts* (9th edn, LBC 1998).
> [2] Timothy Endicott, *Administrative Law* (OUP 2009).
> [3] Gareth Jones, *Goff and Jones: The Law of Restitution* (1st supp, 7th edn, Sweet & Maxwell 2009).
> [4] Leigh Sagar and Jack Burroughs, *The Digital Estate* (2nd edn, Sweet & Maxwell 2022).

If a book consists of more than one volume, the volume number follows the publication details, unless the publication details of the volumes vary, in which case it precedes them, and is separated from the title by a comma. However, if a book comprises multiple volumes the paragraphs of which are numbered consecutively, there is no need to supply a volume number.

> [1] Christian von Bar, *The Common European Law of Torts*, vol 2 (CH Beck 2000).
> [2] WS Holdsworth, *A History of English Law* (Methuen & Co 1965) vol XV, 300.
> [3] Hugh Beale (ed), *Chitty on Contracts* (36th edn, Sweet & Maxwell 2025) para 44.002.

When pinpointing, give the pinpoint after the citation following the guidance in section 3.1.3. By convention, references to paragraph numbers of books are, unlike references to paragraph numbers of judgments, preceded by 'para(s)' and not placed within square brackets.

> [1] Mary Keyes, *Jurisdiction in International Litigation* (Federation Press 2005) 125–26.
> [2] Adrian Briggs, *Agreements on Jurisdiction and Choice of Law* (OUP 2008) para 4.51.

3.2.2 Ebooks

If the ebook provides the same page or paragraph numbers as in the printed publication, cite the ebook as if it was the printed book. If the ebook lacks a printed counterpart, follow the normal book citation form, and include the ebook type/edition before the publisher. If there are no page or paragraph numbers, pinpoint by providing the chapter or section number (or section name, if a number is not provided). It may be helpful to refer to a footnote to indicate the relevant text.

> [1] William Lucy, *Philosophy of Private Law* (Kindle edn, OUP 2007) ch 1, text to n 16.

3.2.3 Edited and translated books

If there is no author, cite the editor or translator as you would an author, adding in brackets after their name '(ed)' or '(tr)', or '(eds)' or '(trs)' if there is more than one.

> [1] Peter Birks and Grant McLeod (trs), *Justinian's Institutes* (Duckworth 1987).
> [2] Jeremy Horder (ed), *Oxford Essays in Jurisprudence: Fourth Series* (OUP 2000).

If the work has an author, but an editor or translator is also acknowledged on the front cover, cite the author in the usual way and attribute the editor or translator at the beginning of the publication information, within the brackets.

> [1] K Zweigert and H Kötz, *An Introduction to Comparative Law* (Tony Weir tr, 3rd edn, OUP 1998).
> [2] HLA Hart, *Punishment and Responsibility: Essays in the Philosophy of Law* (John Gardner ed, 2nd edn, OUP 2008).

3.2.4 Contributions to edited books

When citing a chapter in an edited book, cite the author and the title of the contribution, in a similar format to that used when citing an article, and then give the editor's name, the title of the book in italics and the publication information in brackets.

| author, | 'title' | in editor (ed), | *book title* | (additional information, | publisher | year) |

> [1] John Cartwright, 'The Fiction of the "Reasonable Man"' in AG Castermans and others (eds), *Ex Libris Hans Nieuwenhuis* (Kluwer 2009).
> [2] Justine Pila, 'The Value of Authorship in the Digital Environment' in William H Dutton and Paul W Jeffreys (eds), *World Wide Research: Reshaping the Sciences and Humanities in the Century of Information* (MIT Press 2010).

When pinpointing, give the pinpoint after the citation following the guidance in section 3.1.3. It is unnecessary to indicate the start page of the chapter.

> [1] Donal Nolan and John Davies, 'Torts and Equitable Wrongs' in Andrew Burrows (ed), *Principles of the Law of Obligations* (OUP 2015) para 2.87.
>
> [2] James Edelman and Madeleine Salinger, 'Comity in Private International Law and Fundamental Principles of Justice' in Andrew Dickinson and Edwin Peel (eds), *A Conflict of Laws Companion* (OUP 2021) 325.

3.2.5 Older works

Books published before 1800 commonly have as 'publisher' a long list of booksellers. In such cases, it is appropriate to cite merely the place and year of publication. When citing a recent publication of an older work, it may be appropriate to indicate the original publication year within the brackets and before the publication details of the recent publication.

> [1] Thomas Hobbes, *Leviathan* (first published 1651, Penguin 1985) 268.

3.2.6 Books of authority and institutional works

A small number of older works, such as Blackstone's *Commentaries*, are regarded as books of authority. These works have evolved commonly known abbreviations and citation forms, which should be used in all footnote references to them. A list of some of these works and their abbreviations can be found in section 5.2.3 of the appendix.

> [1] 3 Bl Comm 264.
>
> [2] Co Litt 135a.

Similarly, there are a small number of 'institutional works' which are regarded as formal sources of Scots law. In footnote references, these works should also be referred to by their commonly known abbreviated forms.

> [1] Bankton *Institute* II, 3, 98.
>
> [2] Stair *Institutions* I, 2, 14.

3.2.7 Encyclopedias

Cite an encyclopedia much as you would a book, but excluding the author or editor and publisher and including the edition and year of issue or reissue. Pinpoints come after the publication information following the guidance in section 3.1.3. When an encyclopedia credits an author for a segment, give both the author and the segment title at the beginning of the citation. If citing an online encyclopedia, cite the website address in accordance with the guidance given in section 3.7.1.

> [1] CJ Friedrich, 'Constitutions and Constitutionalism', *International Encyclopedia of the Social Sciences III* (1968) 319.
> [2] Leslie Green, 'Legal Positivism', *The Stanford Encyclopedia of Philosophy* (Fall edn, 2009) <https://perma.cc/9L4R-GYHX>.
> [3] *Halsbury's Laws* (5th edn, 2010) vol 57, para 53.

3.2.8 Dictionaries

Cite entries in hardcopy dictionaries by placing the title of the entry in single inverted commas followed by the title of the dictionary in italics and then the publication details in brackets. It is unnecessary to provide a pinpoint.

> [1] 'no-fault compensation', *Oxford Dictionary of Law* (10th edn, OUP 2022).

Entries in online dictionaries should be cited by citing the website in accordance with section 3.7.1.

3.3 Articles

When citing articles, give the author's name first, followed by a comma. Then give the title of the article within single inverted commas. It should not be italicised. After the title, give the publication information in the following order: (i) year of publication, in square brackets if it identifies the volume, in round brackets if there is a separate volume number; (ii) the volume number if there is one (include an issue number only if, which is unusual, the page numbers begin again for each issue within a volume, in which case put the issue number in brackets immediately after the volume number); (iii) the name of the journal, which should not be italicised, in abbreviated form with no full stops; and (iv) the first page of the article.

> author, | 'title' | [year] | journal abbreviation | first page of article
>
> OR
>
> author, | 'title' | (year) | volume(issue) | journal abbreviation | first page of article

For guidance on journal abbreviations, see section 5.2.1 of the appendix. Abbreviations do vary, so choose an abbreviation and adhere to it throughout your work.

> [1] Paul Craig, 'Theory, "Pure Theory" and Values in Public Law' [2005] PL 440.
> [2] Alison L Young, 'In Defence of Due Deference' (2009) 72 MLR 554.

For pinpoints, put a comma after the first page of the article and follow the guidance in section 3.1.3.

> [1] JAG Griffith, 'The Common Law and the Political Constitution' (2001) 117 LQR 42, 64.
> [2] Jeremy Waldron, 'The Core of the Case Against Judicial Review' (2006) 115 Yale LJ 1346, 1372.

Cite forthcoming articles in the same way as published articles, following the citation with '(forthcoming)'. If volume and/or page numbers are not yet known, simply omit that information.

When citing journal articles which have been published only electronically, give publication details as for articles in hard copy journals to the extent possible, but note that online journals may lack some of the publication elements such as page numbers.

> author, | 'title' | [year] | volume(issue) | journal name or abbreviation |
> OR
> author, | 'title' | (year) | volume(issue) | journal name or abbreviation |

> [1] Graham Greenleaf, 'The Global Development of Free Access to Legal Information' (2010) 1(1) EJLT.
> [2] Dominique Allen and Adriana Orifici, 'What did the COVID-19 Pandemic Reveal about Workplace Flexibility for People with Family and Caring Responsibilities?' [2022] 1 UNSWLJ Forum 1, 4–6.

3.4 Case notes

Treat case notes with titles as if they were journal articles. Where there is no title, use the name of the case in italics instead, and add '(note)' at the end of the citation. Even if not separately cited, the case should be included in the table of cases, citing its best report.

> [1] Andrew Ashworth, '*R (Singh) v Chief Constable of the West Midlands Police*' [2006] Crim LR 441 (note).
> [2] Donal Nolan, 'Nuisance and Privacy' (2021) 137 LQR 1.

3.5 Book reviews

Book reviews should be cited as if they were journal articles save that the text '(book review)' should be added at the end of the citation. Where the review itself has no title, use the name of the book, which should be placed within inverted commas and not italicised.

> [1] AG Guest, 'An Introduction to the Law of Contract' (1961) 24 MLR 658 (book review).
> [2] Donal Nolan, 'Enterprise Liability and the Common Law' (2012) 41 ILJ 370 (book review).

3.6 Working papers

Working papers may be available online on institution websites and on sites such as the *Social Science Research Network* (https://ssrn.com). They should be cited in a similar fashion to electronic journal articles. If a working paper is subsequently published in a journal, cite that in preference to the working paper.

> [1] John M Finnis, 'On "Public Reason"' (2006) Oxford Legal Studies Research Paper 1/2007, 8 <https://perma.cc/2DG8-LUHP>.

3.7 Other secondary sources

Always provide sufficient information to enable the reader to identify the secondary source. Depending on the source, it may be more appropriate to provide the publication date, rather than the year.

3.7.1 Websites

Cite contributions on a website (including blogs) by giving the author's name, the title of the contribution in inverted commas, the name of the website in italics and the date of publication (if known) in round brackets and a link to the website within angled brackets. If no author is identified and it is appropriate to cite an anonymous source, omit the author information. To guard against the risk that a link to a website might cease to be available and/or the website's content might change, it is preferable to generate and cite a persistent link using (for example) Perma.cc rather than the original website address, or a digital object identifier if available. When citing a persistent link or digital object identifier, it is unnecessary to give the date of access, and the latter does not need to be enclosed within angled brackets. If a persistent link or digital object identifier is not available, cite the website page hosting the content and then provide the date of access. Do not cite pdf files or other downloaded content.

> [1] Maximilian Steinbeis, 'A European Network of Constitutional Law Blogs' (*VerfBlog*, 17 March 2015) DOI: 10.17176/20181005-145902-0.
>
> [2] 'When is Human Trafficking Not Human Trafficking? When it Makes a Good Story' (*The Secret Barrister*, 29 November 2022) <https://perma.cc/6548-64JY>.
>
> [3] Cyclefree, 'Is This Really Necessary, Minister?' (*Legal Feminist*, 27 April 2023) <https://perma.cc/3THK-P4AX>.
>
> [4] 'Westminster Update: Economic Crime Bill, Minister Clarifies New Regulatory Objective' (*The Law Society*, 4 July 2023) <https://perma.cc/VXA9-WGB4>.
>
> [5] Geert van Calster, 'Rechtbank Noord Holland on Applicable Law viz a Pig Butchering Scam, Echoing the Classic Difficulty of Distinguishing Contract from Tort' (*GAVC Law*, 15 July 2023) <https://gavclaw.com/2023/07/15/rechtbank-noord-holland-on-applicable-law-viz-a-pig-butchering-scam-echoing-the-classic-difficulty-of-distinguishing-contract-from-tort/> accessed 21 July 2023.

When citing a social media post, provide the time of the post where available and the time zone from which the post is accessed. The username should be cited as it appears on the social media platform. For X (previously known as Twitter) accounts, '@' should be included in the username.

> ¹ @The Criminal Bar (*Twitter*, 26 June 2023, 9:13pm GMT+1) <https://perma.cc/HD6K-3GZQ>.
>
> ² aoc (*Instagram*, 30 June 2023, 1:03am, GMT+4) <https://www.instagram.com/p/CuH0aLrxOFX/?utm_source=ig_web_copy_link&igshid=MzRlODBiNWFlZA==> accessed 21 July 2023.
>
> ³ Joe Biden (*Facebook*, 20 July 2023, 4.06pm GMT+1) <https://www.facebook.com/photo?fbid=314315434506291&set=a.108973695040467> accessed 21 July 2023.

When citing video content on a website, pinpoints should be provided at the end of the citation and before the website address. They should follow the guidance in section 3.1.3.

> ¹ UK Supreme Court, 'Lady Hale's Valedictory Remarks – 18 December 2019' (*YouTube*, 18 December 2019) 42:41–51:17 <https://perma.cc/7YZV-Y43A>.
>
> ² 'Basfar (Respondent) v Wong (Appellant)' (*UK Supreme Court*, 14 October 2021) 2:40:00–2:45:00 <https://perma.cc/NJC5-MNYR>.

3.7.2 Podcasts

When citing a podcast, specify the name of the podcast. This should be followed by the title of the podcast episode in single inverted commas and the full date in brackets. Include the website address if available following the guidance for websites in section 3.7.1. Pinpoints should be provided before the website address. They should follow the guidance in section 3.1.3.

> ¹ Double Jeopardy podcast, 'Episode 27: Dr Bryn Harris – Free Speech, Harm and the Internet' (7 April 2023) 3:40–3:56 <https://podcasts.apple.com/gb/podcast/double-jeopardy/id1633485236?i=1000607857832> accessed 21 July 2023.

3.7.3 Lectures and speeches

When citing lectures and speeches, give the author's name and the title of the lecture or speech in single inverted commas. The name of the lecture or speech, location and date should then be given in brackets. Include website details in accordance with the citation guidance given in section 3.7.1 where available.

> ¹ Stavros Dimas, 'Improving Environmental Quality Through Carbon Trading' (Speech at the Carbon Expo Conference, Cologne, 2 May 2007) <http://europa.eu/rapid/pressReleasesAction.do?reference=SPEECH/07/265> accessed 16 July 2023.
>
> ² Amal Clooney and Philippa Webb, 'Waging Justice in an Age of Authoritarianism' (Lecture at St Hugh's College, Oxford, 15 May 2023).

3.7.4 Interviews

When citing an interview that you conducted yourself, give the name, position and institution (as relevant) of the interviewee and the full date of the interview. If the interview was conducted by someone else, the interviewer's name should appear at the beginning of the citation.

> [1] Interview with Irene Kull, Assistant Dean, Faculty of Law, Tartu University (4 August 2003).
>
> [2] Timothy Endicott and John Gardner, Interview with Tony Honoré, Emeritus Regius Professor of Civil Law, University of Oxford (17 July 2007).

3.7.5 Conference papers

When citing conference papers, give the author's name, the title in single inverted commas and then the title, location and date of the conference in brackets.

> [1] Ben McFarlane and Donal Nolan, 'Remedying Reliance: The Future Development of Promissory and Proprietary Estoppel in English Law' (Obligations III conference, Brisbane, July 2006).

3.7.6 Theses

When citing a thesis, give the author's name, the title of the thesis in italics and then the type of thesis, the university and the year of completion in brackets.

> [1] Javan Herberg, *Injunctive Relief for Wrongful Termination of Employment* (DPhil thesis, University of Oxford 1989).
>
> [2] Ambika Vadehra, *Exploitative Data Harvesting as an Article 102 TFEU Violation* (MPhil thesis, University of Oxford 2021).

3.7.7 Newspaper articles

When citing newspaper or magazine articles, give the author's name, the title of the article in single inverted commas, the name of the newspaper in italics and the date in brackets. If known, give the number of the first page of the article, after the brackets. If the article is sourced from the internet and there is no page number available, cite the article in accordance with the citation guidance for websites given in section 3.7.1.

> [1] Jane Croft, 'Supreme Court Warns on Quality' *Financial Times* (1 July 2010) 3.
>
> [2] Patrick Wintour, 'Russia Accused of "Cynical Brinkmanship" Over Delays to Grain Deal Renewal' *The Guardian* (13 July 2023) <https://www.theguardian.com/world/2023/jul/13/russia-accused-of-cynical-brinkmanship-over-delays-to-grain-deal-renewal> accessed 16 July 2023.

3.7.8 Hansard and parliamentary reports

There are three series of *Hansard*, one reporting debates on the floor of the House of Commons, one debates in the House of Lords and one debates in the Public Bill committees of the House of Commons. When referring to the first two series, cite the House abbreviation ('HL' or 'HC'), followed by 'Deb', then the full date, the volume and the column. Use the abbreviations 'col' or 'cols' for column(s).

> HL Deb | date, | volume, | column
>
> OR
>
> HC Deb | date, | volume, | column

> [1] HC Deb 3 February 1977, vol 389, cols 973–76.
>
> [2] HL Deb 12 November 2009, vol 714, col 893.

Cite debates in the Public Bill committees of the House of Commons with the title of the Bill, followed by 'Deb', followed by the date and the column number. The second example in the following box shows how to cite debates in the old standing committees, which were replaced in 2007.

> [1] Health Bill Deb 30 January 2007, cols 12–15.
>
> [2] SC Deb (A) 13 May 1998, col 345.

When citing reports of select committees of either House, or joint committees of both Houses, give the name of the committee, the title of the report in italics, and then in brackets 'HL' or 'HC', the session and after a comma the paper number and volume number (the latter in roman numerals). For reports of joint committees, cite both the House of Lords and House of Commons paper numbers, in that order.

> [1] Science and Technology Committee, *Genomic Medicine* (HL 2008–2009, 107–I).
>
> [2] Health Committee, *Patient Safety* (HC 2008–2009, 151–I) paras 173–75.
>
> [3] Joint Committee on Human Rights, *Legislative Scrutiny: Equality Bill (second report); Digital Economy Bill* (2009–10, HL 73, HC 425) 14–16.

3.7.9 Command papers

When citing a command paper, begin the citation with the name of the department or other body that produced the paper, and then give the title of the paper in italics, followed by the command paper number and the year in brackets. If additional information is required, insert it within the brackets before the command paper number. The abbreviations preceding a command paper number depend on the year of publication and are as follows:

1833–69 (C (1st series))	1870–99 (C (2nd series))	1900–18 (Cd)
1919–56 (Cmd)	1957–86 (Cmnd)	
1986–2018 (Cm)	2019– (CP)	

> [1] Home Office, *Report of the Royal Commission on Capital Punishment* (Cmd 8932, 1953) para 53.
>
> [2] Department for Children, Schools and Families, *2008 Autumn Performance Report* (Cm 7507, 2008) 54.
>
> [3] Department for International Development, *Eliminating World Poverty: Building our Common Future* (White Paper, Cm 7656, 2009) ch 5.
>
> [4] Department for Science, Innovation & Technology, *A Pro-innovation Approach to AI Regulation* (CP 815, 2023) paras 23–25.

3.7.10 Other government publications

The government publishes a wide variety of documents. These should be cited in accordance with the general principles set out in section 3.1 but some illustrations are as follows:

> [1] Ministry of Justice, *Proposals to Allow the Broadcasting, Filming, and Recording of Selected Court Proceedings* (10 May 2012).
>
> [2] Cabinet Office, 'Ministerial Code' (December 2022).
>
> [3] Competition and Markets Authority, 'Microsoft/Activision Blizzard Merger Inquiry' (6 July 2022).

3.7.11 Law Commission reports and papers

Cite Law Commission reports by giving the title in italics and then the 'Law Com' number and the year in brackets. Do the same with Northern Ireland Law Commission and Scottish Law Commission reports, giving the 'NILC' or 'Scot Law Com' number respectively. Discussion papers and consultation papers should also be cited in this way save that the 'DP' or 'CP' number should be given.

> [1] Law Commission, *Reforming Bribery* (Law Com No 313, 2008) paras 3.12–3.17.
>
> [2] Law Commission, *Privity of Contract: Contracts for the Benefit of Third Parties* (Law Com CP No 121, 1991).
>
> [3] Scottish Law Commission, *Damages for Psychiatric Injury* (Scot Law Com No 196, 2004).
>
> [4] Scottish Law Commission, *Damages for Personal Injury* (Scot Law Com DP No 174, 2022).
>
> [5] Northern Ireland Law Commission, *Bail in Criminal Proceedings* (NILC No 14, 2012).
>
> [6] Northern Ireland Law Commission, *Business Tenancies* (NILC CP No 5, 2010).

3.7.12 Personal communications

When citing personal communications, such as emails and letters, give the author and recipient of the communication, and the date in brackets. If you are yourself the author or recipient of the communication, say 'from author' or 'to author' as appropriate.

> [1] Email from JeffB@amazon.co.uk to author (16 December 2008).
>
> [2] Letter from Gordon Brown to Catherine Ashton (20 November 2009).

3.7.13 Generative artificial intelligence

When citing generative artificial intelligence outputs, cite the artificial intelligence (eg, ChatGPT) as the author. If you have provided instructions to generate the material, specify those instructions in inverted commas. Give the name of the organisation that developed the artificial intelligence followed by the date on which the material was generated in brackets.

> [1] ChatGPT, response to 'Explain how artificial intelligence works', OpenAI (16 July 2023).
>
> [2] ChatGPT, response to 'How to cite ChatGPT in the style of OSCOLA', OpenAI (16 July 2023).

4 International sources

4.1 Treaties

4.1.1 General principles
The components of a treaty citation are as follows:

> treaty title | (parties' names, if bilateral or trilateral) | (date of adoption/signature, date of entry into force) | treaty series identifying information

Treaty title
Include the full title of the treaty, as it appears on its first page. Omit any purely procedural information in the title, such as the date or place of conclusion. Capitalise the first letter of all major words in the title. If appropriate, a short form may be given in brackets at the end of the citation (before any pinpoint) and used in subsequent references.

Parties' names
Do not state the parties to a treaty where there are more than three signatories (ie, a multilateral treaty) or the party names are already expressly stated in the treaty title. Otherwise, state the names of the parties in round brackets, separated by an en-dash.

> [1] International Covenant on Civil and Political Rights (adopted 16 December 1966, entered into force 23 March 1976) 999 UNTS 171 ('ICCPR').
>
> [2] Rehabilitation and Development Co-Operation Agreement (Australia–Nauru) (adopted and entered into force 5 May 1994) [1994] ATS 15.
>
> [3] Bilateral Agreement for the Promotion and Protection of Investments between the Government of the United Kingdom of Great Britain and Northern Ireland and Republic of Colombia (signed 17 March 2010, entered into force 10 October 2014) [2014] UKTS 24 ('UK–Colombia BIT').

Dates of signature, accession, conclusion and/or entry into force
Cite multilateral treaties that are opened for signature generally by providing the date on which the treaty opened for signature. For treaties signed by all State parties (and not open to signature by others), provide the adoption date. For all treaties, then provide the date of entry into force or state if it has not yet entered into force. Draft

treaties should be cited according to the appropriate OSCOLA rules, which will often be those for citing United Nations ('UN') documents (section 4.2).

> [1] International Covenant on Economic, Social and Cultural Rights (opened for signature 19 December 1966, entered into force 3 January 1976) 993 UNTS 3 ('ICESCR').
>
> [2] Convention Relating to the Status of Refugees (adopted 28 July 1951, entered into force 22 April 1954) 189 UNTS 137 ('Refugee Convention').
>
> [3] United Nations Convention on Jurisdictional Immunities of States and Their Property (adopted 2 December 2004, opened for signature 17 January 2005, not yet in force) 44 ILM 803.

Treaty series

Where produced in multiple treaty series, cite the treaty series in the following order of preference: *United Nations Treaty Series* ('UNTS'), *League of Nations Treaty Series* ('LNTS') or *Consolidated Treaty Series* ('CTS'); an official treaty series of a State party, such as the *UK Treaty Series* ('UKTS') or *Australian Treaty Series* ('ATS'); another international treaty series, such as the *Pacific Islands Treaty Series* ('PITS'), *European Treaty Series* ('ETS'), *Organization of American States Treaty Series* ('OAS Treaty Series') or *British and Foreign State Papers* ('BFSP'). Where the first page of the treaty is included in the citation, cite the first page of the Final Act (if that appears before the text of the treaty itself), but do not include the words 'Final Act'. An example is the Convention relating to the Status of Refugees: the Final Act appears at 189 UNTS 137 whereas the text of the treaty begins at 189 UNTS 150.

Where the treaty series is arranged by volume number, give the volume number before the treaty series abbreviation and the first page of the treaty.

> [1] Protocol Relating to the Status of Refugees (adopted 31 January 1967, entered into force 4 October 1967) 606 UNTS 267, art 2.
>
> [2] Convention between Great Britain, Japan, Russia and the United States Requesting Measures for the Preservation and Protection of Fur Seals in the North Pacific Ocean (signed 7 December 1911) 214 CTS 80.

Where the treaty series is organised by year, provide the year in square brackets before the abbreviation for the treaty series, followed by the first page of the treaty or treaty number.

> [1] Agreement between the Government of the United Kingdom of Great Britain and Northern Ireland and the Government of the United Arab Emirates for the Promotion and Protection of Investments (signed 8 December 1992, entered into force 15 December 1993) [1994] UKTS 24 ('UK–UAE BIT').

For treaty series organised by order of deposit of the treaty, cite the sequential order after the treaty series abbreviation.

> [1] Convention on Cybercrime (opened for signature 23 November 2001, entered into force 1 July 2003) ETS No 185.

Pinpoints
Pinpoint to article numbers, preceded by a comma unless following a closing bracket.

> ¹ United Nations Convention on the Law of the Sea (opened for signature 10 December 1982, entered into force 16 November 1994) 1833 UNTS 3 ('UNCLOS') art 46.
> ² Slavery Convention (adopted 25 September 1926, entered into force 9 March 1927) 60 LNTS 253, art 5.
> ...
> ¹³ UNCLOS, art 101.

4.1.2 Treaty reservations and declarations

Cite a declaration or reservation available on the *United Nations Treaty Collection* ('UNTC') by stating the depository, treaty title, location of the information on the treaty page (for example, 'Declarations and Reservations') and the submitting State. Cite information contained in an endnote by pinpointing to 'End Note [number]'. Provide website addresses in accordance with section 3.7.1.

> ¹ UNTC Depositary, Status of Treaties, ICCPR, Declarations and Reservations, Australia <https://perma.cc/UCZ2-7XX3>.
> ² UNTC Depositary, Status of Treaties, ICCPR, Declarations and Reservations, Australia, End Note 14, <https://perma.cc/UCZ2-7XX3>.

For treaty reservations and declarations contained elsewhere, follow the general principles in section 3.1.

> ¹ Council of Europe, 'Reservations and Declarations for Treaty No 005 – Convention for the Protection of Human Rights and Fundamental Freedoms (ETS No 005)' <https://perma.cc/8W47-G7Z2>.
> ² Organisation of American States, 'American Convention on Human Rights "Pact of San Jose, Costa Rica" (B-32): Signatories and Ratifications' <https://perma.cc/CFR6-KETD>.

4.1.3 WTO/GATT agreements and related official documents

Constitutive treaties for the World Trade Organization ('WTO') should be cited in accordance with section 4.1.1.

> ¹ Marrakesh Agreement Establishing the World Trade Organization (opened for signature 15 April 1994, entered into force 1 January 1995) 1867 UNTS 3, annex 1A ('GATT 1994').

Cite official WTO and General Agreement on Tariffs and Trade ('GATT') documents (except Appellate Body reports, panel reports and arbitrator decisions, which should be cited in accordance with section 4.3.4) as follows:

> document title | (document description, if available) | document number | (date)

Where the document does not include a full date, cite as much of it as appears in the document. Include any adoption date as shown in the examples below. Only include a document description where it appears in the document. Pinpoint to page numbers, paragraph numbers, articles and parts as applicable.

> [1] Agreement on Agriculture, WTO Doc LT/UR/A-1A/2 (15 April 1994) art 2.
>
> [2] Cuba – Article XV:6 (Request for Extension of Waiver) WTO Doc WT/L/1003 (18 October 2021) [2.9].
>
> [3] Generalized System of Preference (Notification by Finland, Addendum) GATT Doc L/3694/Add.9 (2 January 1980).

Where a document is reproduced in the *Basic Documents and Selected Documents* ('BISD'), cite the BISD after the full date. The abbreviation 'BISD' should be followed by the volume or supplement number (together with an 'S' if a supplement) and the first page of the document, separated by an oblique stroke.

> [1] Declaration on Trade Measures Taken for Balance-of-Payments Purposes, GATT Doc L/4904 (3 December 1979, adopted 28 November 1979) BISD 26S/205, 208.

4.2 United Nations documents

4.2.1 UN Charter

Cite the Charter of the United Nations, without reference to a treaty series or conference proceedings, as follows:

> [1] UN Charter, art 33.

4.2.2 General principles

Generally, cite UN documents as follows:

> body, | 'title' | (date) | unique identifying information
>
> OR
>
> body | resolution number (date) | unique identifying information

Abbreviate names such as 'United Nations' to 'UN', 'UN Security Council' to 'UNSC', 'UN General Assembly' to 'UNGA' and 'International Law Commission' to 'ILC'. Also abbreviate 'Resolution' to 'Res', 'Number' to 'No' and 'Document' to 'Doc'. State the full names of lesser known or more specialised UN organs or bodies. Examples given below are illustrative only; authors should determine when an abbreviation is appropriate for their particular audience. Note that if the document is a resolution, the date given should be that of the resolution, which is not necessarily that of the UN document. Short titles may be given at the end of citations and used in subsequent references.

> [1] UNSC Res 1373 (28 September 2001) UN Doc S/RES/1373.
>
> [2] HRC, 'Concluding Observations on the Sixth Periodic Report of Hungary' (9 May 2018) CCPR/C/HUN/CO/6.
>
> [3] UNGA Res 2625(XXV) (24 October 1970) UN Doc A/RES/2625(XXV) annex ('Friendly Relations Declaration').
>
> [4] ILC, 'Third Report on General Principles of Law by Marcelo Vázquez-Bermúdez, Special Rapporteur' (18 April 2022) UN Doc A/CN.4/753.

Italicise the title of a UN document only if it has been published as a book (ie, if it has an ISBN), in which case it is unnecessary to provide the UN document number and the citation should conform to the principles in section 3.1.

> [1] Operations Evaluation Department, *China: An Evaluation of World Bank Assistance* (The World Bank 2005).

4.2.3 United Nations Yearbooks and Official Records

Cite a UN yearbook or UN official records as follows:

> body/author, | 'heading or title of the section' | [year] OR (year) | volume number(issue OR part) | publication name | first page

Provide the year of publication in square brackets if the yearbook is organised by year and round brackets if organised by volume. Abbreviate the name of the yearbook.

> [1] UN Office for Disarmament Affairs, 'Implementation of the Intermediate-Range Nuclear Forces Treaty' (2018) 43(II) UN Disarmament YB 20.
>
> [2] UN Office for Ocean Affairs and the Law of the Sea, 'Fiji, Indonesia, Mauritius and Philippines: Draft Articles Relating to Archipelagic States' (1973/1974) III UNCLOS III OR 226.

4.2.4 International Law Commission materials

Cite final texts adopted by the ILC, such as draft conclusions, principles and articles, that have been annexed in full to a UN General Assembly resolution in accordance with section 4.2.2. Otherwise, cite such texts as they appear in the Yearbook of the International Law Commission ('YBILC') in accordance with section 4.2.3. Where such texts have not yet been published in the Yearbook, cite them as they appear in the ILC's Report to the General Assembly.

> [1] UNGA Res 56/83, 'Articles on Responsibility of States for Internationally Wrongful Acts' (12 December 2001) UN Doc A/56/83, annex ('ARSIWA') art 5.
>
> [2] ILC, 'Draft Conclusions on Identification of Customary International Law' [2018] II(II) YBILC 90.
>
> [3] ILC, 'Draft Conclusions on Identification and Legal Consequences of Peremptory Norms of General International Law (*Jus Cogens*)' (2022) UN Doc A/77/10, Draft Conclusion 2.

When citing the commentary to such texts, pinpoint to page numbers. Where there are multiple paragraphs of commentary on a single page, give both page numbers and paragraph numbers. Further identifying information can be provided in brackets after the pinpoint.

> [1] ILC, 'Draft Articles on Prevention and Punishment of Crimes Against Humanity' (2019) UN Doc A/74/10, 28–47 (commentary to Draft Article 2).
>
> [2] ILC, 'Draft Principles on Protection of the Environment in Relation to Armed Conflicts, with Commentaries' (2022) UN Doc A/77/10, 105 para 3 (commentary to Draft Principle 4).

4.2.5 United Nations agencies

Cite documents published by UN agencies according to the general principles in section 4.2.2. Replace the UN document number with the appropriate alternative identifying information. Where no specific identifying information is provided in the document, cite the document in accordance with the general principles in section 4.5.1.

> [1] World Health Assembly, 'Cancer Prevention and Control in the Context of an Integrated Approach' (31 May 2017) Doc No WHA70.12.
>
> [2] World Food Programme, 'Global Report on Food Crises – 2022' (2022) <https://perma.cc/J6P4-2MHL>.

4.2.6 United Nations treaty bodies

Structure citations of decisions or views adopted by UN treaty bodies as follows:

> *title* | (type of decision or document) | treaty body communication number | (date of decision)

The title of the decision should comprise the surname of the complainant and the respondent State, separated by an italicised '*v*'. Where the complainant in an individual communication is different from the alleged victim, use the name of the alleged victim. Abbreviate treaty body names. Provide the full date of decision, which may be different from the date of the document.

> [1] *Cherguit v Algeria* (Views) HRC Communication No 2828/2016 (27 March 2020) [7.3].
>
> [2] *Osmani v Serbia* (Decision) CAT Communication No 261/2005 (8 May 2009).
>
> [3] *Sacchi v Argentina* (Decision) CRC Communication No 104/2019 (22 September 2021) [5.5].

Cite other documents of UN treaty bodies in accordance with the general principles in section 4.2.2.

4.3 International cases and decisions

4.3.1 International Court of Justice and Permanent Court of Justice
Cite reported decisions of the International Court of Justice ('ICJ') or Permanent Court of International Justice ('PCIJ') as follows:

> *case name* | *(parties' names* OR *Advisory Opinion)* | (phase) | (type of decision) | [year] | report information | first page

Case names
Give the name of the case in full, omitting words such as 'Case', 'Cases' and 'Case Concerning', when it is first mentioned in the text or footnotes. Case names can be shortened when cited subsequently. Thus, '*Arrest Warrant of 11 April 2000*' can be shortened to '*Arrest Warrant*'.

> ¹ *Arrest Warrant of 11 April 2000 (DRC v Belgium)* (Judgment) [2002] ICJ Rep 3.
> ² *Legal Status of Eastern Greenland (Denmark v Norway)* (Judgment) [1933] PCIJ Ser A/B No 53.
> ...
> ⁷ *Arrest Warrant* (n 1) [59].

Parties' names or Advisory Opinion
Retain the way in which the parties' names are separated in the judgment as, in contentious cases, this indicates whether the dispute has been brought before the Court by a unilateral application or by special agreement. For the former, party names are separated by the abbreviation '*v*' and for the latter, by an oblique stroke.

> ¹ *Corfu Channel (UK v Albania)* (Merits) (Judgment) [1949] ICJ Rep 4.
> ² *Frontier Dispute (Burkina Faso/Niger)* (Judgment) [2013] ICJ Rep 44 [108]–[111].

For decisions in Advisory Opinion proceedings, the words 'Advisory Opinion' should appear in brackets following the case name.

> ¹ *Legal Consequences of the Separation of the Chagos Archipelago from Mauritius in 1965 (Advisory Opinion)* [2019] ICJ Rep 95.

Phase
If there are official phases for proceedings, cite the phase in which the decision has been made, as identified in the decision.

> ¹ *LaGrand (Germany v USA)* (Provisional Measures) (Order) [1999] ICJ Rep 9.
>
> ² *Application of the International Convention on the Elimination of All Forms of Racial Discrimination (Qatar v UAE)* (Preliminary Objections) (Judgment) [2021] ICJ Rep 71.
>
> ³ *Land, Island and Maritime Frontier Dispute (El Salvador/Honduras, Nicaragua intervening)* (Application for Permission to Intervene) (Judgment) [1990] ICJ Rep 92.

Type of decision or document

Identify the type of decision or court document in round brackets after the case name and phase, if any. Where the decision is an Advisory Opinion, do not repeat '(Advisory Opinion)'. Where advisory proceedings result in more than one advisory opinion or when citing a document in such proceedings that is not an advisory opinion, give information regarding the decision or document type as if it related to contentious proceedings.

> ¹ *Fisheries Jurisdiction (UK v Iceland)* (Interim Measures of Protection) (Order) [1972] ICJ Rep 12.
>
> ² *Legal Consequences of the Separation of the Chagos Archipelago from Mauritius in 1965 (Advisory Opinion)* (Order) [2017] ICJ Rep 282.
>
> ³ *Interpretation of Peace Treaties with Bulgaria, Hungary and Romania (Advisory Opinion)* (Second Phase) [1950] ICJ Rep 221.

Report information

Where the decision has been reported in the *ICJ Reports* or *PCIJ Series*, provide the report series after the year in short form. It should not be italicised. For PCIJ decisions, include the series letter(s) and number(s).

> ¹ *Factory at Chorzów (Germany v Poland)* (Merits) (Judgment) [1928] PCIJ Ser A No 17.
>
> ² *Free Zones of Upper Savoy and the District of Gex (Switzerland v France)* (Judgment) [1932] PCIJ Ser A/B No 46.

Unreported decisions and other case documents

Where a judgment is not yet reported, provide the case number followed by the date of the document in brackets.

> ¹ *Certain Iranian Assets (Islamic Republic of Iran v USA)* (Merits) (Judgment) ICJ Case No 164 (30 March 2023) [55]–[73].
>
> ² *Allegations of Genocide under the Convention on the Prevention and Punishment of the Crime of Genocide (Ukraine v Russia)* (Declaration of Intervention of Latvia) ICJ Case No 182 (19 July 2022) [55].

Separate and dissenting opinions

When referring to a particular passage of a dissenting opinion, separate opinion or declaration, state the document type in a footnote citation in brackets after the pinpoint together with the name of the judge. If the opinion contains paragraph numbers independent of the main judgment, the page number should be included in the pinpoint and separated from the first page of the judgment by a comma. Where the opinion contains page numbers and paragraph numbers independent of the main judgment, as may be the case in an unreported decision, pinpoint to paragraph numbers only.

> [1] *Arrest Warrant of 11 April 2000 (DRC v Belgium)* (Judgment) [2002] ICJ Rep 3, 80 [58] (Separate Opinion of Judges Higgins, Kooijmans and Buergenthal).
>
> [2] *Legality of the Threat or Use of Nuclear Weapons (Advisory Opinion)* [1996] ICJ Rep 226, 443 (Dissenting Opinion of Judge Weeramantry).
>
> [3] *Certain Iranian Assets (Islamic Republic of Iran v USA)* (Merits) (Judgment) ICJ Case No 164 (30 March 2023) [12] (Separate Opinion of Judge Tomka).

4.3.2 International Tribunal for the Law of the Sea

Cite decisions and case documents of the International Tribunal for the Law of the Sea ('ITLOS') in the same format as ICJ or PCIJ materials (section 4.3.1).

> [1] *M/V 'Virginia G' (Panama/Guinea-Bissau)* (Judgment) [2014] ITLOS Rep 4.
>
> [2] *Dispute Concerning Delimitation of the Maritime Boundary Between Ghana and Côte d'Ivoire in the Atlantic Ocean (Ghana/Côte d'Ivoire)* (Judgment) [2017] ITLOS Rep 4.
>
> [3] *'Enrica Lexie' (Italy v India)* (Provisional Measures) (Order) [2015] ITLOS Rep 182.
>
> [4] *Dispute Concerning Delimitation of the Maritime Boundary Between Mauritius and Maldives in the Indian Ocean (Mauritius/Maldives)* (Judgment) ITLOS Case No 28 (28 April 2023).

4.3.3 International Criminal Court and ad hoc criminal tribunals

Cite decisions of the International Criminal Court ('ICC') or international(ised) criminal tribunals as follows:

> *case name* | (type of decision) | case/document number | (date)

Case names should consist of the words 'Prosecutor' or 'Co-Prosecutors' and the defendant's surname, separated by the abbreviation '*v*'.

> [1] *Prosecutor v Tadić* (Decision on the Defence Motion for Interlocutory Appeal on Jurisdiction) IT-94-1 (2 October 1995).
>
> [2] *Prosecutor v Bemba* (Decision on the Confirmation of Charges) ICC-01/05-01/08 (15 June 2009).
>
> [3] *Prosecutor v Taylor* (Decision on Immunity from Jurisdiction) SCSL-03-01-I-059 (31 May 2004).
>
> [4] *Co-Prosecutors v Nuon Chea et al* (Judgment) 002/19-09-2007/ECCC/TC (16 November 2018) [115].

4.3.4 WTO/GATT decisions

Cite WTO or GATT panel reports, Appellate Body reports and arbitral decisions as follows:

> *case name* | (document description) | document identifying information | (date(s))

The document description should refer to the type of decision, as described in the document. In the document identifying information, include the body and document number in abbreviated form. The date(s) provided should be the circulation date and adoption date (if any).

> [1] *Korea – Measures Affecting Imports of Fresh, Chilled and Frozen Beef* (Appellate Body Report) WTO Doc Nos WT/DS161/AB/R and WT/DS169/AB/R (circulated 11 December 2000, adopted 10 January 2001) [161].
>
> [2] *Canada – Import Restrictions on Ice Cream and Yoghurt* (Panel Report) GATT Doc No L/6568 (circulated 27 September 1989, adopted 5 December 1989) [8].
>
> [3] *Brazil – Export Financing Programme for Aircraft* (Art 22.6 DSU Arbitration Decision) WTO Doc No WT/DS46/ARB (circulated 28 August 2000, authorisation to retaliate 12 December 2000) [2.7].

4.3.5 International arbitral and other tribunal decisions

Cite an arbitral or other tribunal decision as follows:

> *case name* | (parties' names) | (phase) | (type of decision or document) | tribunal or administering body | document identifying information | (date)

Abbreviate the name of the tribunal or administering body according to conventional practice. For example, the 'International Centre for the Settlement of Investment Disputes' should appear as 'ICSID' and 'Permanent Court of Arbitration' should appear as 'PCA' alongside the case number as identifying information.

> [1] *The 'Enrica Lexie' Incident (Italy v India)* (Merits) (Award) PCA Case No 2015-28 (21 May 2020) [840].
>
> [2] *CMS Gas Transmission Company v Argentina Republic* (Merits) (Award) ICSID Case No ARB/01/8 (12 May 2005).
>
> [3] *Bendone–Derossi International v Iran* (Interim Award) Iran–US CTR Award No ITM 40-375-1 (7 June 1984) 5.
>
> [4] *G v Eurocontrol* (Judgment) ILO Administrative Tribunal Judgment No 4471 (9 November 2021) [24].
>
> [5] *Rofman (No 2) v IBRD* (Preliminary Objection) (Judgment) World Bank Administrative Tribunal Decision No 681 (18 November 2022).

Citing a reported version of a decision in publications such as the *International Law Reports* ('ILR'), ILM or *Reports of International Arbitral Awards* ('RIAA') may also be appropriate, especially for older decisions. The components of a reported citation are as follows:

case name | *(parties' names)* | (phase) | (type of decision or document) | (year) | volume | report series | first page

> [1] *Nuremberg International Military Tribunal* (Judgment) (1947) 41 AJIL 172.
>
> [2] *Alabama Claims of the United States of America against Great Britain* (Award) (1872) XXIX RIAA 125 ('*Alabama Claims Arbitration*').
>
> [3] *Starrett Housing Corporation v Iran* (Interlocutory Award) (1983) 4 Iran–US CTR 122.

4.3.6 Other materials of international courts and tribunals

Cite case-related documents in accordance with the rules for unpublished ICJ judgments in section 4.3.1.

> [1] *Elliott Associates LP (United States) v Korea* (Claimant's Amended Statement of Claim) PCA Case No 2018-51 (4 April 2019) [23].
>
> [2] *Gabčíkovo-Nagymaros Project (Hungary/Slovakia)* (Memorial of the Republic of Hungary) ICJ Case No 92 (2 May 1994) [3.26].

Cite versions of case-related documents published in official reports such as the *ICJ Pleadings* series as follows:

case name | *(parties)* | volume number | official report series | first page

> [1] *Aerial Incident of July 27 1955 (Israel v Bulgaria)* ICJ Pleadings 530.

Cite all other international court or tribunal documents according to the general principles in section 4.2.2.

> [1] ICC, 'Request to all states parties to the Rome Statute for the arrest and surrender of Omar Al Bashir' (6 March 2009) Doc No ICC-02/05-01/09-7.
>
> [2] ICC, 'Observations of DRC authorities on the decision of Pre-Trial Chamber II of the International Criminal Court requesting for observations on Omar Al Bashir's visit to the Democratic Republic of the Congo' (official court trans, 27 March 2014) Doc No ICC-02/01-190-AnxII-tENG, 7.

References to basic documents of international courts and tribunals, such as Rules of Court ('RoC'), Rules of Procedure ('RoP') or Rules of Procedure and Evidence ('RPE') should consist of the body, and the title of the document, without reference to adoption information.

¹ ICJ RoC, art 7(1).
² ICJ PD XIII.
³ HRC RoP, r 97.
⁴ ICC RPE, r 12(1)(a).
⁵ ICJ Statute, art 38(1)(b).

4.4 Regional materials

4.4.1 European Union legislation

Official notices of the EU are carried in the *Official Journal of the European Union* ('OJ'). The OJ citation is given in the order: year, OJ series, number/page. The letter 'L' denotes the legislative series (the 'C' series contains EU information and notices and the 'S' series, invitations to tender for public contracts). A space should appear between the letters 'OJ' and the letter denoting the series (eg, 'S') but not between the letter denoting the particular series and the number/page.

When citing EU treaties and protocols, give the title of the legislation, including amendments if necessary, followed by the year of publication, the OJ series reference and the issue and page numbers as follows:

> legislation title | [year] | OJ series | issue/first page

Older treaties were published in the C series. With notable exceptions, such as the Lisbon Treaty, legislation is now published in the L series.

> ¹ Protocol to the Agreement on the Member States that do not fully apply the Schengen acquis – Joint Declarations [2007] OJ L129/35.
>
> ² Consolidated Version of the Treaty on European Union [2020] OJ C202/1 ('Maastricht Treaty').

Cite EU Regulations, Directives, Decisions, Recommendations and Opinions as follows:

> legislation name, including type of legislation and number | title | [year] | OJ L issue/first page

The legislation name should be given as it appears on the first page of the document. Note that, for legal acts published in the L series of the OJ from 1 January 2015, the document's number consists of the domain (given in round brackets) followed by the year of publication and the document's sequential number. And for legal acts published from 1 October 2023, instead of the issue/first page the publication date should be supplied.

> ¹ Council Directive 2002/60/EC of 27 June 2002 laying down specific provisions for the control of African swine fever and amending Directive 92/119/EEC as regards Teschen disease and African swine fever [2002] OJ L192/27.
>
> ² Council Regulation (EC) No 1984/2003 of 8 April 2003 introducing a system for the statistical monitoring of trade in bluefin tuna, swordfish and big eye tuna within the Community [2003] OJ L295/1.
>
> ³ Council Regulation (EU) 2015/159 of 27 January 2015 amending Regulation (EC) No 2532/98 concerning the powers of the European Central Bank to impose sanctions [2015] OJ L27/1.
>
> ⁴ Commission Decision (EU, Euratom) 2015/444 of 13 March 2015 on the security rules for protecting EU classified information [2015] OJ L72/53.
>
> ⁵ Regulation (EU) 2015/2283 of the European Parliament and of the Council of 25 November 2015 on novel foods, amending Regulation (EU) No 258/97 of the European Parliament and of the Council and repealing Regulation (EC) No 258/97 of the European Parliament and of the Council and Commission Regulation (EC) No 1852/2001 [2015] OJ L327/1.
>
> ⁶ Regulation (EU) 2024/1083 of the European Parliament and Council of 11 April 2024 establishing a common framework for media services in the internal market and amending Directive 2010/13/EU (European Media Freedom Act) [2024] OJ L 17.4.2024.

Short forms and pinpoints

Give EU legislation its full name on first citation. In subsequent citations, a short form may be used or, in a footnote, simply the document type and number (using 'Reg' and 'Dir' as abbreviations).

> ¹ Regulation (EC) No 593/2008 of the European Parliament and of the Council of 17 June 2008 on the law applicable to contractual obligations [2008] OJ L177/6 ('Rome I').
>
> ² Council Regulation (EC) No 1206/2001 of 28 May 2001 on cooperation between the courts of the Member States in the taking of evidence in civil or commercial matters [2001] OJ L174/1.
>
> …
>
> ⁶ Rome I, art 6.
>
> …
>
> ¹⁴ Council Reg 1206/2001, art 17(1).

Older EU legislation

For the years 1952–72 (when there was no English edition of the *Journal Officiel*), refer where possible to the Special Edition of the OJ, abbreviated to 'OJ Spec Ed'.

> ¹ Council Regulation (EEC) 1017/68 applying rules of competition to transport by rail, road and inland waterway [1968] OJ Spec Ed 302.

4.4.2 Court of Justice of the European Union and General Court decisions
The typical components of a citation for an EU court decision are:

| case number | *case name* | European Case Law Identifier |

Case number
Since 1989, EU court cases have been numbered according to whether they were registered at the Court of Justice of the European Union ('CJEU') or the General Court ('GC') and given the prefix 'C-' (for CJEU cases) or 'T-' (for GC cases). Prior to December 2009, the CJEU was called the 'Court of Justice' ('ECJ') and the General Court was called the Court of First Instance ('CFI'). Judgments from the Civil Service Tribunal, which was established in 2005 and ceased to exist in 2016, are prefixed 'F-'. Do not add a 'C-' to pre-1989 cases.

European Case Law Identifier
Since 2014, all EU court judgments have been given a European Case Law Identifier ('ECLI'). An ECLI, for decisions of EU courts, consists of the following elements: the code 'EU'; the abbreviation corresponding to the court which delivered the decision; the year of the decision; and the ordinal number of the decision. Note that an ECLI has been assigned to all decisions delivered by EU courts since 1954 and to the opinions of the Advocates General. All such material should now be cited using the appropriate ECLI.

> [1] Case C-403/03 *Schempp v Finanzamt* EU:C:2005:446 [19].
> [2] Case T-344/99 *Arne Mathisen AS v Council* EU:T:2002:174.

In the ECLI provided in the exemplar *Schempp* citation given above, 'EU' indicates that it is a decision delivered by an EU court. (For decisions of national courts, the code corresponding to the relevant Member State should appear instead of 'EU'.) 'C' indicates that the decision was delivered by the CJEU. '2005' indicates that the decision was delivered in 2005. '446' indicates that it is the 446th ECLI assigned in respect of the year in question.

Opinions of Advocates General
Cite an opinion of an Advocate General with the ECLI specific to the opinion followed by the words 'Opinion of AG [surname]', separated by a comma. Pinpoints should be to 'point(s)' rather than 'para(s)', preceded by a comma.

> [1] Case C-189/16 *Zaniewicz-Dybeck v Pensionsmyndigheten* EU:C:2017:329, Opinion of AG Wathelet, point 51.

4.4.3 European Commission materials
Decisions of the European Commission in relation to competition law and mergers are to be treated as if they were cases for the purposes of citation. Give the names of

the parties (or the commonly used short form) in italics, the case number in brackets, the Commission Decision number (where available) and the OJ report as follows:

> *case name* | (case number) | Commission Decision number | [year] | OJ L issue/first page

> [1] *Alcatel/Telettra* (Case IV/M.042) Commission Decision 91/251/EEC [1991] OJ L122/48.
> [2] *Georg Verkehrsorgani v Ferrovie dello Stato* (Case COMP/37.685) Commission Decision 2004/33/EC [2004] OJ L11/17.

When citing European Commission documents (such as proposals and action plans), provide the name of the body that produced the document, followed by the document title in single inverted commas and the COM number. Describe the document type in brackets after the title if appropriate.

> [1] European Commission, 'Proposal for a Council Decision on the conclusion, on behalf of the European Community, of the Protocol on the Implementation of the Alpine Convention in the Field of Transport (Transport Protocol)' COM (2008) 895 final, ch I, art 3.
> [2] European Commission, 'Action Plan on consumer access to justice and the settlement of disputes in the internal market' (Communication) COM (96) 13 final.

4.4.4 European Court of Human Rights decisions

For decisions of the European Court of Human Rights ('ECtHR'), the components of a typical citation are:

> *case name* | (phase) | (type of decision or document) | [chamber/committee] | court | application number | (date)

Include information on the stage of proceedings, if multiple, and decision or document type after the case name in brackets. Where the case was heard by the Grand Chamber of the Court, add '[GC]' after the name, phase and decision or document type and '[Committee]' where the judgment or decision has been given by a three-judge Committee.

> [1] *Broniowski v Poland* (Merits) (Judgment) [GC] ECtHR App No 31443/96 (22 June 2004).
> [2] *Tatuyev v Russia* (Judgment) [Committee] ECtHR App No 3333/08 (21 July 2020).
> [3] *Ukraine and the Netherlands v Russia* (Jurisdiction and Admissibility) (Decision) [GC] ECtHR App Nos 8019/16, 43800/14 and 28525/20 (25 January 2023) [826].

Cite Advisory Opinions as above but with any relevant identifying information, such as a request number, instead of the application number. If the words 'Advisory Opinion' already appear in the case name, do not include them again.

> [1] *Advisory Opinion Concerning the Recognition in Domestic Law of a Legal Parent-Child Relationship Between a Child Born Through a Gestational Surrogacy Arrangement Abroad and the Intended Mother* [GC] ECtHR Request No P16-2018-001 (10 April 2019) [25]–[34].

4.4.5 European Commission of Human Rights decisions

Cite decisions and reports of the European Commission of Human Rights, which ceased to function in 1998, by case name, year of decision (in brackets) and reference to the *Decisions and Reports of the Commission*, *Yearbook of the ECHR* or, for decisions prior to 1974, the *Collection of Decisions of the Commission* report. If available, a reference to a report of the decision in the *European Human Rights Reports* is also acceptable but should be followed by the words '(Commission Decision)'. For unreported decisions, give the application number followed by the words 'Commission Decision' and the date of the decision in brackets.

> [1] *X v Netherlands* (1971) 38 CD 9.
> [2] *Council of Civil Service Unions v UK* (1987) 10 EHRR 269 (Commission Decision).
> [3] *Simpson v UK* (1989) 64 DR 188.
> [4] *P v UK* App No 13473/87 (Commission Decision, 11 July 1988).
> [5] *Ward v UK* (1966) YB 9.

4.4.6 Inter-American Court of Human Rights decisions

Cite Inter-American Court of Human Rights decisions as reported in the *Inter-American Court of Human Rights Series* with reference to the series and number particulars.

> [1] *Juridical Condition and Rights of Undocumented Migrants* (Advisory Opinion) [2003] IACtHR Ser A No 18.
> [2] *Olivera Fuentes v Peru* (Judgment) [2023] IACtHR Ser C No 484.

4.4.7 Other regional courts and tribunals

Structure citations to the decisions of other regional courts and tribunals as follows:

> *case name* | (phase) | (type of decision or document) | court/tribunal | case/application number | (date)

> [1] *Sangare v Mali* (Judgment) ACHPR App No 007/2019 (23 June 2022) [44].

4.4.8 Other materials of regional bodies

Regional treaties should be cited in accordance with section 4.1.1. Cite other documents of regional bodies as follows:

> author, | 'title', | document number or unique identifying information | (date)

> [1] African Commission on Human and Peoples' Rights, 'Principles and Guidelines on the Right to a Fair Trial and Legal Assistance in Africa', Doc No DOC/OS(XXX)247 (2003).
>
> [2] African Union and African Union Development Agency-NEPAD, *Second Continental Report on the Implementation of Agenda 2063* (AUC & AUDA-NEPAD, 2022).
>
> [3] Association of Southeast Asian Nations, 'ASEAN Human Rights Declaration' (adopted 19 November 2012).
>
> [4] Association of Southeast Asian Nations, 'Bangkok Declaration on Combating Marine Debris in ASEAN Region' (22 June 2019).

4.5 Other international sources

4.5.1 General principles

For other international sources, follow the general principles for citing secondary sources (section 3.1). If a source has an ISBN, cite it like a book. Generally, cite sources that do not have ISBNs in a similar way, but with the title styled as for journal articles (no italics, and in single inverted commas). Additional information may include a document number, a document description, a date or session of adoption and any other information that may help the reader to locate the source. The publisher may be a government body or an organisation. It is also possible that no publisher is identifiable. If a source is only available online, cite it in accordance with the guidance given in section 3.7.1.

> [1] US Bureau of Oceans and International Environmental and Scientific Affairs, 'Limits in the Seas, People's Republic of China: Maritime Claims in the South China Sea' (Study No 150, US Department of State, January 2022).
>
> [2] Jean-Marie Henckaerts and Louise Doswald-Beck, *Customary International Humanitarian Law* (CUP 2005) vol 1 ('ICRC Customary Study').

4.5.2 International Yearbooks

Cite International Yearbooks in the same way as journals (section 3.3). If the Yearbook uses roman numerals for volume numbers, use roman numerals. Where documents are printed in English and French, cite the version used.

> [1] Robert Jennings, 'The Role of the International Court of Justice' (1997) 68 BYIL 10.
>
> [2] 'Le Conseil de L'Europe: Principales activités pour l'année 1999' (1999) XLVII Annuaire Européen (C de E) 1.

4.5.3 International Law Association and Institut de Droit International documents

Cite the Institut de Droit International ('IIL') Yearbook as if it were a UN yearbook (section 4.2.3).

> [1] 'Observations de M. A. S. de Bustamante' (1912) 25 Institut de Droit International Yearbook 218, 221.

Cite resolutions, reports and other publications of the International Law Association ('ILA') and IIL according to the general principles for citing other international sources (section 4.5.1).

> [1] ILA, 'Baselines under the International Law of the Sea' (Interim Report, 2014).
>
> [2] Institut de droit International, 'Human Rights and Private International Law' (Resolution, 4th Commission, 4 September 2021).
>
> [3] Campbell McLachlan, 'Equality of Parties before International Investment Tribunals' (Preparatory Report of the Special Rapporteur, 18th Commission of the Institut de droit International, 2018).

4.5.4 Collected Courses of the Hague Academy of International Law

Abbreviate 'Recueil des Cours de l'Académie de Droit International' to 'Rd C'. Cite the volume year (which is not necessarily the same as the publication year). Prior to 1995, volumes ('tomes') were divided into parts, signified by roman numerals. Omit the roman numeral for the part and cite the year and volume instead. The final component of the citation is the first page of the article.

> [1] Edward McWhinney, 'Judicial Settlement of Disputes: Jurisdiction and Justiciability' (1990) 221 Rd C 9.

4.5.5 International law digests

Cite particular sections of international law digests by providing the title or topic of the section in single inverted commas, followed by the year (if given) and/or volume number (in roman numerals if used in the publication). Use '§' to indicate the section referred to (if arranged by section symbols and numbers). If the digest is not arranged by section symbols and numbers, include the first page of the section after the title of the digest. Pinpoint to page numbers.

> [1] 'Aviation' (1968) 9 Whiteman Digest Intl Law §4, 321.
>
> [2] 'Territorial Regimes and Related Issues' (2021) Digest of US Practice Intl Law 494, 502.
>
> [3] 'Peaceful Settlement of Disputes' (1981–88) 3 Cumulative Digest of US Practice Intl Law §2, 3190.

4.5.6 Max Planck Encyclopedias of International Law

Cite entries in the Max Planck Encyclopedias of International Law according to the principles for encyclopedias (section 3.2.7). For online entries, provide the year the entry was last updated. No website link is necessary.

> [1] Erika de Wet and Michael Wood, 'Collective Security', *Max Planck Encyclopedia of Public International Law* (2013) para 6.
>
> [2] Cedric Ryngaert, 'Horizontal Complementarity', *Max Planck Encyclopedia of International Procedural Law* (2018) para 17.

5 Appendix

5.1 Guide to medium neutral citations

5.1.1 United Kingdom

Supreme Court	[Year] UKSC number
House of Lords	[Year] UKHL number
Privy Council	[Year] UKPC number

5.1.2 England and Wales

Court of Appeal (Civil Division)	[Year] EWCA Civ number
Court of Appeal (Criminal Division)	[Year] EWCA Crim number
Court of Protection	[Year] EWCOP number
Family Court	[Year] EWFC number
High Court, Administrative Court	[Year] EWHC number (Admin)
High Court, Admiralty Court	[Year] EWHC number (Admlty)
High Court, Commercial Court	[Year] EWHC number (Comm)
High Court, Chancery Division	[Year] EWHC number (Ch)
High Court, Family Division	[Year] EWHC number (Fam)
High Court, King's Bench Division	[Year] EWHC number (KB)
High Court, Patents Court	[Year] EWHC number (Pat)
High Court, Queen's Bench Division	[Year] EWHC number (QB)
High Court, Technology and Construction Court	[Year] EWHC number (TCC)

5.1.3 Scotland

Court of Session, Inner House	[Year] CSIH number
Court of Session, Outer House	[Year] CSOH number
Court of Criminal Appeal	[Year] HCJAC number
High Court of Justiciary (sitting as a trial court)	[Year] HCJT number

Sheriff Appeal Court (Civil)	[Year] SAC Civ number
Sheriff Appeal Court (Criminal)	[Year] SAC Crim number
Sheriff Court	[Year] SC, followed by a court identifier and judgment number

5.1.4 Northern Ireland

Court of Appeal	[Year] NICA number
High Court of Justice, King's Bench Division	[Year] NIKB number
High Court of Justice, Queen's Bench Division	[Year] NIQB number
High Court of Justice, Family Division	[Year] NIFam number
High Court of Justice, Chancery Division	[Year] NICh number
Crown Court	[Year] NICC number
Masters' Decisions	[Year] NIMaster number

5.1.5 Tribunals

Competition Appeal Tribunal	[Year] CAT number
Employment Appeal Tribunal	[Year] UKEAT number
First-tier Tribunal (Health, Education and Social Care Chamber)	[Year] UKFTT number (HESC)
First-tier Tribunal (Social Entitlement Chamber)	[Year] UKFTT number (SEC)
First-tier Tribunal (War Pensions and Armed Forces Compensation Chamber)	[Year] UKFTT number (WPAFCC)
Special Immigration Appeals Commission	[Year] UKSIAC number
Upper Tribunal (Administrative Appeals Chamber)	[Year] UKUT number (AAC)
Upper Tribunal (Immigration and Asylum Chamber)	[Year] UKUT number (IAC)
Upper Tribunal (Lands Chamber)	[Year] UKUT number (LC)
Upper Tribunal (Tax and Chancery Chamber)	[Year] UKUT number (TCC)

5.2 Abbreviations

5.2.1 Abbreviations of the names of law reports, journals and treaty series

Define abbreviations in a list at the beginning of a book or thesis (section 1.6.1). The abbreviations provided below for law reports and journals do not need to be defined. For abbreviations that are not in these lists, use any preferred abbreviation given in the *Cardiff Index of Legal Abbreviations* (www.legalabbrevs.cardiff.ac.uk); failing that, use any of the possible abbreviations given in the *Cardiff Index*; and, failing that, use the following terms to develop an abbreviation:

Criminal	Crim	Quarterly	Q
European	Eur	Report(s)	Rep(s)
International	Intl	Review	Rev
Journal	J	University	U
Law or Legal	L	Yearbook	YB

Law reports

All England Law Reports	All ER
All England Law Reports (Commercial Cases)	All ER (Comm)
British Company Law Cases	BCC
Business Law Reports	Bus LR
Civil Procedure Reports	CP Rep
Consumer and Trading Law Cases	CTLC
Common Market Law Reports	CMLR
Criminal Appeal Reports	Cr App R
Criminal Appeal Reports (Sentencing)	Cr App R (S)
Current Law Yearbook	CLY
English Reports	ER
Environmental Law Reports	Env LR
Estates Gazette	EG
Family Law Reports	FLR
Financial Times Law Reports	FTLR
Fleet Street Reports	FSR
Immigration Appeal Reports	Imm AR
Industrial Cases Reports	ICR
Industrial Relations Law Reports	IRLR
Information Technology Law Reports	Info TLR
Justiciary Cases	JC
Journal of Planning and Environment Law	JPL
Justice of the Peace Reports	JP
Law Reports	AC, KB, QB, Ch, Fam, P
Law Society Gazette	LS Gaz
Lloyd's Law Reports	Lloyd's Rep

Lloyd's Law Reports Banking	Lloyd's Rep Bank
Lloyd's Law Reports Financial Crime	Lloyd's Rep FC
Lloyd's Law Reports Insurance and Reinsurance	Lloyd's Rep IR
Lloyd's Law Reports Medical	Lloyd's Rep Med
Lloyd's Law Reports Professional Negligence	Lloyd's Rep PN
Local Government Reports	LGR
Property and Compensation Reports	P & CR
Public and Third Sector Law Reports	PTSLR
Reports of Patent Cases	RPC
Road Traffic Reports	RTR
Scots Law Times	SLT
Scottish Civil Law Reports	SCLR
Scottish Criminal Case Reports	SCCR
Session Cases (Scotland)	SC
Simon's Tax Cases	STC
Tax Cases	TC
Weekly Law Reports	WLR
Weekly Law Reports (Daily Case Summaries)	WLR (D)

International reports

Basic Documents and Selected Documents	BISD
Collection of Decisions of the Commission	CD
Decisions and Reports of the Commission	DR
Dispute Settlement Reports	DSR
European Court Reports	ECR
European Human Rights Reports	EHRR
International Court of Justice Reports	ICJ Rep
International Court of Justice Pleadings Series	ICJ Pleadings
International Human Rights Reports	IHRR
International Tribunal for the Law of the Sea Reports	ITLOS Rep
International Law Reports	ILR
International Legal Materials	ILM
Iran-US Claims Tribunal Reports	Iran-US CTR
Permanent Court of International Justice Reports	PCIJ Rep
Reports of International Arbitral Awards	RIAA
Reports of Judgments and Decisions	ECHR

Journals

American Journal of International Law	AJIL
British Tax Review	BTR
British Yearbook of International Law	BYIL
Common Market Law Review	CML Rev
Cambridge Law Journal	CLJ

Conveyancer	Conv
Current Legal Problems	CLP
Criminal Law Review	Crim LR
EC Bulletin	EC Bull
European Competition Law Review	ECLR
Estates Gazette	EG
European Journal of International Law	EJIL
European Intellectual Property Review	EIPR
European Industrial Relations Review	EIRR
European Law Review	EL Rev
Industrial Law Journal	ILJ
International Law Quarterly	ILQ
International and Comparative Law Quarterly	ICLQ
International Journal of Law in Context	Int JLC
Journal of Business Law	JBL
Journal of Corporate Law Studies	JCLS
Journal of Competition Law and Economics	JCL & E
Journal of Environmental Law	JEL
Journal of International Economic Law	J Intl Econ L
Journal of Planning and Environmental Law	JPEL
Lloyd's Maritime & Commercial Law Quarterly	LMCLQ
Law Quarterly Review	LQR
Legal Studies	LS
Law Society Gazette	LS Gaz
Modern Law Review	MLR
New Law Journal	NLJ
Official Journal of the Union	OJ
Oxford Journal of Legal Studies	OJLS
Oxford University Commonwealth Law Journal	OUCLJ
Public Law	PL
Recueil des Cours de l'Académie de Droit International	Rd C
Solicitors' Journal	SJ

Treaty series

Australian Treaty Series	ATS
British and Foreign State Papers	BFSP
Consolidated Treaty Series	CTS
European Treaty Series	ETS
International Legal Materials	ILM
League of Nations Treaty Series	LNTS
Organization of American States Treaty Series	OAS Treaty Series
Pacific Islands Treaty Series	PITS
UK Treaty Series	UKTS
United Nations Treaty Series	UNTS

5.2.2 Abbreviations used in legal historical works

Ames Foundation	AF
Bracton's Note Book	BNB
Curia Regis Rolls	CRR
Easter term	Pas
Hilary term	Hil
Michaelmas term	Mich
Publications of the Selden Society	SS
plea number	pl
Rolls Series	RS
Rotuli Curiae Regis	RCR
Trinity term	Trin
Yearbook	YB

5.2.3 Abbreviations of the titles of books of authority

Blackstone, *Commentaries on the Law of England*	Bl Comm
Bracton, *On the Laws and Customs of England*	Bracton
Brooke, *La Graunde Abridgement*	Brooke Abr
Coke, *Commentary upon Littleton*	Co Litt
Coke, *Institutes of the Laws of England*	Co Inst
Fitzherbert, *La Graunde Abridgement*	Fitz Abr
Fitzherbert, *La Novel Natura Brevium*	Fitz NB
Glanvill, *Treatise on the Laws and Customs of England*	Glanvill
Hawkins, *A Treatise on the Pleas of the Crown*	Hawk PC
Hale, *The History of the Pleas of the Crown*	Hale PC

5.2.4 Abbreviations in case names

Attorney General	A-G
Anonymous	Anon
Area Health Authority	AHA
British Broadcasting Corporation	BBC
Borough Council	BC
Brothers	Bros
County Council	CC
Company	Co
Commissioner/Commissioners	Comr/Comrs
Co-operative	Co-op
Corporation	Corp
Crown Prosecution Service	CPS
District Council	DC
deceased	decd
Department	Dept
Director of Public Prosecutions	DPP

European Communities	EC
Executor	Exor
Executrix	Exrx
Great Britain	GB
Health Authority	HA
Her/His Majesty	HM
Her/His Majesty's Revenue Commissioners	HMRC
Incorporated	Inc
The King or Queen	R
London Borough Council	LBC
liquidation	liq
Limited	Ltd
New Zealand	NZ
others	ors
public limited company	plc
Proprietary	Pty
Railway	Rly
Rural District Council	RDC
South Africa	SA
Urban District Council	UDC
United Kingdom	UK
United States	US
United States of America	USA
Vice-Chancellor	V-C

5.2.5 Abbreviations of common words and phrases in footnotes

Advocate General	AG
affirmed	affd
appendix	app
article/articles	art/arts
Cambridge University Press	CUP
cf	compare
chapter/chapters	ch/chs
chapter/chapters (of statutes)	c/cc
clause/clauses	cl/cls
column/columns	col/cols
compiler/compilers	comp/comps
Directive	Dir
Document (for UN Documents etc)	Doc
edition	edn
editor/editors	ed/eds
and following	ff
footnote/footnotes (internal to the work)	n/nn
footnote /footnotes (external to the work)	fn/fns
for example	eg

manuscript/manuscripts	MS/MSS
margin number	mn
number/numbers	no/nos
Oxford University Press	OUP
paragraph/paragraphs	para/paras
part/parts	pt/pts
Regina/Rex	R
regulation/regulations	reg/regs
reversed	revd
rule/rules	r/rr
schedule/schedules	sch/schs
section/sections	s/ss
subsection/subsections	sub-s/sub-ss
subparagraph/subparagraphs	subpara/subparas
supplement/supplements	supp/supps
that is	ie
translator/translators	tr/trs
University Press	UP
volume/volumes	vol/vols

5.2.6 Abbreviations of international institutions and bodies

African Court on Human and Peoples' Rights	ACHPR
Committee on Economic, Social and Cultural Rights	CESCR
Committee on the Elimination of Discrimination against Women	CEDAW
Committee on the Elimination of Racial Discrimination	CERD
Committee on the Rights of the Child	CRC
Committee against Torture	CAT
Court of Justice of the European Union	CJEU
European Court of Human Rights	ECtHR
European Union	EU
Hague Conference on Private International Law	HCCH
Human Rights Committee	HRC
Inter-American Court of Human Rights	IACtHR
International Centre for the Settlement of Investment Disputes	ICSID
International Court of Justice	ICJ
International Commercial Court	ICC
International Committee of the Red Cross	ICRC
International Criminal Court	ICC
International Criminal Tribunal for the Former Yugoslavia	ICTY
International Labour Organization	ILO

International Law Association	ILA
International Law Commission	ILC
International Tribunal for the Law of the Sea	ITLOS
Organization of American States	OAS
Organization for African Unity	OAU
Permanent Court of Arbitration	PCA
Permanent Court of International Justice	PCIJ
United Nations	UN
United Nations General Assembly	UNGA
United Nations High Commissioner for Refugees	UNHCR
United Nations Human Rights Council	UNHRC
United Nations Security Council	UNSC
World Health Organization	WHO
World Trade Organization	WTO

5.3 Guides for other jurisdictions

Australia

Australian Guide to Legal Citation (4th edn, Melbourne University Law Review Association 2021) <https://law.unimelb.edu.au/mulr/aglc/about> accessed 18 April 2023.

Canada

McGill Law Journal, *Canadian Guide to Uniform Legal Citation* (10th edn, Carswell 2023).

Canadian Citation Committee, 'The Preparation, Citation and Distribution of Canadian Decisions' <https://lexum.com/ccc-ccr/preparation/en/> accessed 27 May 2023.

France

Follow the form of citation and presentation generally adopted by the *Recueil Dalloz*.

Germany

Hildebert Kirchner, *Abkürzungsverzeichnis der Rechtssprache* (11th edn, de Gruyter 2024).

Hong Kong

Wilson Lui, 'Hong Kong Citation of Legal Authorities and Materials' <www.hkclam.org> accessed 1 November 2025.

Ireland

OSCOLA Ireland, 'OSCOLA Ireland 2016' <www.legalcitation.ie> accessed 27 May 2023.

Israel

'The Uniform Citation Rules' (1989) 39 The Lawyer and (1998) 44 The Lawyer (in Hebrew).

New Zealand

Geoff McLay, Christopher Murray and Jonathan Orpin, *New Zealand Law Style Guide* (3rd edn, Thomson Reuters 2018).

South Africa

Follow the style used in the *South African Law Journal*.

United States

Association of Legal Writing Directors and Darby Dickerson (eds), *ALWD Citation Manual: A Professional System of Citation* (7th edn, Aspen Publishers 2021).

The Bluebook: A Uniform System of Citation (22nd edn, Harvard Law Review Association 2025).

5.4 Other useful sources

Emily Allbon, *Legal Research: A Practitioner's Handbook* (3rd edn, Wildy, Simmonds & Hill Publishing 2019).
Jeremy Butterfield, *The New Fowler's Modern English Usage* (4th edn, OUP 2015).
Derek French, *How to Cite Legal Authorities* (Blackstone 1996).
Bryan A Garner, *A Dictionary of Modern Legal Usage* (3rd edn, OUP 2011).
Bryan A Garner, *The Elements of Legal Style* (2nd edn, OUP 2002).
Ernest Gowers, *Plain Words* (Rebecca Gowers ed, rev edn, Penguin 2015).
Anne Waddingham (ed), *New Hart's Rules: Oxford Style Guide* (2nd edn, OUP 2014).
Charlotte Harrison and Amanda Millmore, *Glanville Williams: Learning the Law* (18th edn, Sweet & Maxwell 2025).

Index

Abbreviations
  books of authority, 68
  Cardiff Index of Legal
    Abbreviations, 65
  case names, 14, 68–69
  Command papers, 42
  footnotes, 5–6, 69–70
  ibid; *supra*; *infra*; *ante*; *id*; *op cit*;
    loc cit; *contra*, 8
  indicators, 5–6
  international institutions and
    bodies, 70–71
  journals, 37, 66–67
  law reports, 65–66
  legal historical works, 68
  lists of abbreviations, 11,
    65–71
  primary legislation, 26
  punctuation, 8
  secondary legislation, 30
  treaty series, 67
  words and phrases, 69–70
Acts, *see* **UK legislation**
Articles
  forthcoming articles, 38
  journal abbreviations, 37, 66–67
  newspaper articles, 41
  online journals, 38
  working papers, 39
Artificial intelligence, *see* **Generative artificial intelligence**
Assimilated EU law, 29
Authors' names
  articles, 37
  bibliographies, 12–13
  books, 34
  footnotes, 33
  punctuation, 8
  secondary sources, 33
  subsequent citations, 6
  surnames, 7

Bibliographies, 12–13
Bills, 27
  Northern Ireland, 29
  Scotland, 28
  Wales, 28
Blogs, *see* **Websites and blogs**
Books, 34
  authored books, 34–35
  books of authority, 36, 68
  citation in footnotes, 5, 7

  contributions to edited books, 35–36
  dictionaries, 37
  e-books, 35
  edited and translated books, 35
  encyclopaedias, 36–37
  institutional works, 36
  International Standard Book
    Number, 34
  older works, 36
  pinpoints/page numbers, 34
  publication information, 34
  volume numbers, 34
Brexit
  assimilated EU law, 29

**Cardiff Index of Legal
  Abbreviations,** 65
Case notes, 38
Case numbers, 19
  EU law, 11, 58
    European Commission materials,
      58–59
  international arbitral tribunals, 54
  international law
    unreported decisions, 52
Cases (England and Wales)
  case names
    abbreviations, 15
    Attorney General's references, 17
    corporate status, 15
    descriptions, 15
    different name/different law reports, 17
    different name/different stages, 17
    individuals as parties, 15
    judicial review applications, 17
    multiple parties, 15
    short forms, 15–17
    variations, 17
  citing cases, 3–4
    subsequent citation, 6
  courts, 19–20
  ecclesiastical courts, 22
  general principles, 14–15
  judges' names, 20–22
  law reports, 18–19
  neutral citations, 14, 18
  older cases, 22–23
  pinpoints, 20
  subsequent history, 22
  unreported cases, 19
  year of judgment, 15, 17
  yearbook references, 23

Cases (European Commission
    of Human Rights), 60
Cases (European Court of Human
    Rights), 59–60
Cases (European Union), 58
Cases (Northern Ireland), 25
Cases (international), 32
    Inter-American Court of Human
        Rights, 60
    International arbitral decisions,
        54–55
    International Court of Justice, 51–53,
        55–56
    International Criminal Court, 53
    International Tribunal for the Law of
        the Sea, 53
    other regional courts/tribunals,
        60–61
    Permanent Court of Justice, 51–53
    WTO/GATT decisions, 54
Cases (Scotland), 23–24
Chapters in books, 33, 35
Citation
    abbreviations, 5–6
        see also Abbreviations
    cases, 3–4
    footnotes, 3
    foreign jurisdictions, 31–32
    foreign sources, 9
    general advice
        consideration for reader, 1
        consistency, 1
    legislation, 4–5
    primary sources, 3
    subsequent citations
        authors' names, 7
        books, 5, 7
        cases, 6
        examples, 6–7
        legislation, 6–7
        secondary sources, 5
        two works by same author, 7
    see also Neutral citations
Civil Procedure Rules (CPR), 30
Command papers, 42
Conference papers, 41
County Court Rules, 30
Court of Justice of the EU (CJEU)
    case numbers, 58
    European Case Law Identifier, 58
    opinions of Advocate General, 58
Courts
    abbreviations, 19–20
    citation pre-1865, 19–20
    neutral citation, 18, 19–20,
        63–64
    use of brackets in citations, 18, 19
Criminal Procedure Rules
    (CrPR), 30
Cross-references, 7–8

Editors, 33
Electronic sources, 33
    lectures and speeches, 40
    online journals, 38
    online papers, 41
    podcasts, 40
    websites, 33, 36, 37, 39–40
    working papers, 39
Emails, 44
Encyclopaedias, 36–37
EU law
    assimilated EU law, 29
    Official Journal, 56
    official notices, 56
    older legislation, 57
    pinpoints, 57
    Regulations; Directives; Decisions;
        Recommendations; Opinions ..., 56–57
    short forms, 57
    treaties and protocols, 56
    see also European Court of Justice
EU legal sources
    case law, 58
    European Commission Decisions
        and documents, 58–59
    legislation, 29, 57
    *Official Journal of the European
        Communities*, 56
European Commission
    COM numbers, 59
    documents, 58–59
European Commission of Human
    Rights (EComHR), 60
European Court of Human Rights
    (ECtHR), 59–60
Explanatory notes to statutes, 27

Family Procedure Rules (FPR), 30
Footnotes
    abbreviations in, 5–6, 69–70
    authors' names, 33
    cases, 3, 5
    cross-references, 7–8
    footnote markers, 3, 7–8,
        9–10, 33
    *ibid; supra; infra; ante; id; op cit;
        loc cit; contra*, 8
    judges' names, 20–21
    legislation, 4–5
    order of sources, 5
    punctuation, 3, 5
    quotations, 3, 9–10
    secondary sources, 5
    subsequent citations, 6–7
    words and phrases in, 69–70
Foreign sources
    citation, 9, 31 –32
    guides, 71–72
    primary sources, 31–32
Foreign words, 8–9

General Agreement on Tariffs and
    Trade (GATT), 47–48, 54
Generative artificial intelligence
    citation, 44

Hansard, 42
House of Lords (HL)
    abbreviations, 19–20
    Hansard, 42
    House of Lords' Bills, 27
    neutral citations, 18, 23–24, 63

Incorporated Council of Law
    Reporting (ICLR), 18–19
Indicators, 5–6
Institut de Droit International (IDI),
    61–62
Inter-American Court of
    Human Rights (IACtHR), 60
International Centre for the
    Settlement of Investment
    Disputes (ICSID), 54–55
International Court of Justice (ICJ)
    Advisory Opinions, 51
    case names, 51
    dissenting opinions, 52–53
    document type, 52
    parties, 51
    phases of proceedings, 51–52
    reports and report series, 52
    separate opinions, 52–53
    type of decision, 52
    unpublished ICJ judgments, 55
    unreported decisions, 52
International Criminal Court (ICC), 53
International law
    general principles, 61
    Hague Academy of International
        Law, 62
    Institut de Droit International, 61–62
    International Law Association,
        61–62
    International Law Commission
        commentary, 50
        draft conclusions; principles;
            articles ..., 49
        Yearbook of the ILC, 49
    international law digests, 62
    International Yearbooks, 61
    Max Planck Encyclopedias of
        International Law, 62
    *Recueil des Cours de l'Académie
        de Droit International,* 62
    treaties
        dates: signature; accession;
            conclusion; entry into force ...,
            45–46
        declarations, 47
        general principles, 45
        parties, 45
        pinpoints, 47
        regional treaties, 60–61
        reservations, 47
        treaty series, 46–47
        treaty titles, 45
    UN agencies, 50
    UN documents
        Charter, 48
        general principles, 48–49
        UN Yearbooks, 49
        UN official records, 49
    UN treaty bodies, 50
    WTO treaties
        GATT, 47–48
International Law Association (ILA), 61–62
International Law Commission (ILC)
    commentary, 50
    draft conclusions; principles; articles ..., 49
    Yearbook of the ILC, 49
International Standard Book Number
    (ISBN), 34
International Tribunal for the
    Law of the Sea (ITLOS), 53
International Yearbooks, 61
Interviews, 41

Journal articles, 37–38
Judges' names
    England and Wales, 20–22
    footnote citation, 22
    forenames, 21
    Northern Ireland, 25
    pinpoints, 21
    Scotland, 24
    subsequent elevation, 21
    territorial qualifications, 21

Latin gadgets
    *ibid; supra; infra; ante; id; op cit;
        loc cit; contra,* 8
Law Commission reports, 43
Law reports
    England and Wales, 17
        abbreviations, 65–66
        All England Law Reports, 19
        Appeal Cases, 14
        best report, 18–19
        case numbers, 19
        citation, 17
        English Reports, 22
        headnotes, 18
        heavily edited reports, 19
        Law Reports, 17–19
        specialist reports, 19
        Weekly Law Reports, 8, 19
    foreign law report series, 31
    Northern Ireland
        Northern Ireland Law Reports, 25
        Irish Reports, 25
        Irish Times Reports, 25

Scotland, 23
   brackets, 24
   Scots Law Times, 24
   Scottish Civil Law Reports, 24
   Scottish Criminal Case Reports, 24
   Session Cases, 24
Legislation
   primary legislation
      citation, 4–5
      EU law, 29
      Northern Ireland, 28–29
      Scotland, 28
      UK, 25–27
      Wales, 27–28
Letters, 44

Max Planck Encyclopedias of International Law, 62

Neutral citations, 3
   abbreviations, 63–64
   courts, 16, 18, 19–20, 63–64
   England and Wales, 14, 18
   judgment number, 18
   Northern Ireland, 25, 64
   numbered paragraphs, 18
   Scotland, 23–24, 63–64
   single report/more than one judgment, 18
   transcripts of judgments, 18
   tribunals, 64
   unreported judgments, 19
   year of judgment, 18
Newspaper articles, 41
Northern Ireland
   bills, 29
   cases, 25
   judges' names, 25
   law reports
      Northern Ireland Law Reports, 25
      Irish Reports, 25
      Irish Times Reports, 25
   neutral citations, 25, 64
      see also **Neutral citations**
   primary legislation, 28–29
   secondary legislation, 31
Numbers, ranges of, 8

Online journals, 38

Parliamentary committees, 42
Periodicals, 37–38
Permanent Court of Arbitration (PCA), 54–55
Permanent Court of Justice (PCJ)
   Advisory Opinions, 51
   case names, 51
   dissenting opinions, 52–53
   document type, 52
   parties, 51
   phases of proceedings, 51–52

reports and report series, 52
separate opinions, 52–53
type of decision, 52
unreported decisions, 52
Personal communications, 44
Pinpoints/page numbers, 4, 6
   articles, 37
   cases
      England and Wales, 20
      Scotland, 24
   court identifiers, 19–20
   dictionaries, 37
   e-books, 35
   edited books, 36
   encyclopaedias, 36–37
   EU law, 57, 58
   European Case Law Identifier, 58
   international law
      International Court of Justice, 52–53
      International Law Commission materials, 50
      international law digests, 62
      treaties, 47
      WTO/GATT, 48
   page numbers, 20
   paragraph numbers, 20
   podcasts, 40
   secondary sources, 33, 34
   video content on websites, 40
Podcasts, 40
   pinpoints, 33
Practice Directions (PDs), 30
Punctuation
   abbreviations, 8
   authors' names, 8
   bibliographies, 12–13
   case citations, 31
   commas, 9
   footnotes, 3, 5
   general advice, 1
   indicators, 5–6
   names of statutes, 25
   pinpoints in cases, 20
   quotations, 9
   secondary sources
      authored books, 34

Quotations, 9–10

Ranges of numbers and years, 8
Recueil des Cours de l'Académie de Droit International, 62
Regional courts and tribunals, 60
Rules of court, 30
Rules of the Supreme Court (RSC), 30

Scotland
   bills, 28
   cases, 23–24

judges' names, 24
law reports, 23
   brackets, 24
   Scots Law Times, 24
   Scottish Civil Law Reports, 24
   Scottish Criminal Case Reports, 24
   Session Cases, 24
neutral citations, 23–24, 63–64
pinpoints/page numbers, 24
primary legislation, 28
Scottish Law Commission, 43
secondary legislation, 31
secondary sources
   articles, 37–38
   bibliographies, 12–13
   book reviews, 38
   books, 34–37
   case notes, 38
   citation, 5
   command papers, 42–43
   conference papers, 41
   date of access, 39
   edited books, 35–36
   electronic sources, 33
   email, 44
   encyclopaedias, 36–37
   footnotes, 5
   foreign sources, 9
   generative artificial intelligence, 44
   Hansard, 42
   institutional works, 36
   International Standard Book Number, 34
   interviews, 41
   journals, 37–38
   Law Commission reports, 43
   lectures and speeches, 40
   letters, 44
   newspaper articles, 41
   older works, 36
   online sources, 39–40
   page numbers, 33, 34
   parliamentary papers, 42
   periodicals, 37–38
   personal communications, 44
   pinpoints, 33, 34
   podcasts, 40
   publication date, 39
   speeches, 40
   subsequent citations, 34
   theses, 41
   titles, 33
   translated books, 35
   web addresses, 36, 39, 40
   websites, 39–40
   working papers, 39
Social media, 33, 39–40
Statutes, *see* **UK primary legislation**
Statutory instruments, *see* **UK secondary legislation**
Subsequent citations
   authors' names, 7
   books, 7
   cases, 6, 16
   EU law, 57
   international treaties, 45
   legislation, 6–7, 25–26
   secondary sources, 5, 34
   two works by same author, 7

Tables of cases, 11–12, 38
Tables of legislation, 11, 12
Theses, 41
Translators, 35

UK primary legislation
   assimilated EU law, 29
   bills, 27
      Northern Ireland, 29
      Scotland, 28
      Wales, 28
   chapter number, 26
   citing legislation, 4–5
      subsequent citation, 6
   explanatory notes, 27
   names of statutes, 25
   Northern Ireland, 28–29
   older statutes, 26
   parts of statutes, 26
   regnal year, 26
   royal assent, 26
   Scotland, 28
   Wales, 27–28
UK secondary legislation
   abbreviation, 29–30
   citation, 29–30
   consecutive numbering, 29
   Northern Ireland, 31
   parts of statutory instruments, 30
   practice directions, 30
   rules of court, 30
   Scotland, 31
   SI numbers, 29–30
   secondary legislation, 29–30
   statutory rules and orders, 30
   subsequent citation in footnote, 6–6
   Wales, 31
United Nations
   UN agencies, 50
   UN documents
      Charter, 48
      general principles, 48–49
      UN official records, 49
      UN Yearbooks, 49
   UN treaty bodies, 50
Unreported cases, 19
   international law, 52

Wales
   primary legislation, 27
   secondary legislation, 31

Websites, 33, 39–40
  international treaties, 47
  newspaper articles, 41
  online dictionaries, 37
  online encyclopedias, 36
  working papers, 39
Working papers, 39
World Trade Organization (WTO)
  GATT, 47–48, 54

Yearbook references
  abbreviations, 68
  British Yearbook of International Law, 66
  Current Law Yearbook, 65
  cases from England and Wales, 23
  European Commission of Human Rights, 60
  Institut de Droit International Yearbook, 61–62
  International Law Association, 61–62
  International Law Commission, 49
  International Yearbooks, 61
  UN Yearbooks, 49
Years, ranges of, 8